11/21
POEMS
$5

D0948354

LOUIS MACNEICE : SCEPTICAL VISION

Terence Brown

LOUIS MACNEICE : SCEPTICAL VISION

'Through art we can know another's
view of the universe.'
Marcel Proust, *Maxims*

GILL AND MACMILLAN · DUBLIN
BARNES & NOBLE BOOKS · NEW YORK
a division of Harper & Row Publishers, Inc.

First published in 1975

Gill and Macmillan Limited
2 Belvedere Place
Dublin 1
and internationally through
association with the
Macmillan Publishers Group
Published in the U.S.A. 1975 by
Harper & Row Publishers, Inc.
Barnes & Noble Import Division

Extracts from Louis MacNeice, *The Strings are False* used by
permission of the Executors of Louis MacNeice, and David
Higham Associates Limited.
Extracts from *The Collected Poems of Louis MacNeice,* edited
by E. R. Dodds © The Estate of Louis MacNeice 1966, re-
printed by permission of Faber and Faber Limited (G.B.), and
Oxford University Press, Inc. (U.S.).

Gill & Macmillan SBN: 7171 0698 5
Barnes & Noble ISBN: 06 490734 1

Printing History: 5 4 3 2 1

Printed in Great Britain
by Bristol Typesetting Co Ltd Barton Manor Bristol.

Contents

Acknowledgments

ACKNOWLEDGMENTS are due to Professor Philip Edwards who encouraged me to undertake literary research; to Mrs. Harden Rodgers-Jay, Professor Brendan Kennelly, Professor J. K. Walton and Dr. T. R. Henn, who read my typescript at various stages and made useful comments. Acknowledgments are also due to the late George McCann and to his wife Mercy Hunter who told me much of Louis MacNeice and his feelings about Ireland. Special gratitude is due to Mrs Hedli MacNeice who gave me access to unpublished materials and was helpful in every way, and to Professor E. R. Dodds who read my typescript at a late stage, making valuable suggestions. I am also grateful to Mrs MacNeice and Professor Dodds for permission to quote from the works of Louis MacNeice.

To my wife, Suzanne, whose critical encouragement has been invaluable, thanks are also due.

Foreword

ANTHONY THWAITE'S comments on MacNeice in his book
Contemporary English Poetry for a long time represented critical
orthodoxy about this poet:

> His work is very readable, he is never boring, he is an excel-
> lent craftsman, and has many of the virtues of a good
> journalist—a 'reporter of experience' with sharp, vivid, precise
> phrases. But he seldom has much depth or penetration, and
> his general lightness of tone is more that of the professional
> entertainer than it is with Auden.[1]

It is such a view of MacNeice that I wish to challenge in this
book, for it seems to me that MacNeice has been much misrepresented by many of his critics. It has all too easily been
assumed that the surface brilliance of his poems represents the
whole of his achievement. Few critics have bothered to concern
themselves with the ideas in MacNeice's poems, assuming that
a pose of decent, contemporary fair-minded liberalism was the
poet's only creed. Few have seemed aware of the complexities
of his most refined sensibility.

In this book I intend to take MacNeice seriously, both as poet
and as thinker. I am encouraged in this enterprise by some
critics' beginning awareness of the hidden depths of MacNeice's
poetry and thought.[2] In a conversation with MacNeice's friend,
the Ulster painter, George McCann, shortly before his death in
1967, I learnt that MacNeice felt through his life, especially
in his later years, that the critics had misunderstood his work,
since he considered it much more metaphysical than they seemed
aware.

I will argue that the central determining factor in MacNeice's
poetry and thought, far from being a decent, liberal, but rather

commonplace agnosticism, was a tense awareness of fundamental questions, rooted in philosophical scepticism. It is this basic scepticism which, I feel, has confused critics. They have too easily assumed that its result—a lack of simple dogmatic creed—is of the same kind as their own liberal confusion. It was deeper, more rigorously held and applied, than they perhaps realise.

To accomplish this aim I shall examine MacNeice's characteristic themes, attitudes and responses (in Part I) showing that the basis of these is an underlying, rarely departed from, scepticism. Chapter one will deal with specifically Romantic themes of quest, forsaken or lost home, and briefly glimpsed ideals including ideal love. It will show, through extensive references to specific poems, that the themes are treated with self-denial and undercutting scepticism. In this MacNeice shares the common modern attitude to Romantic dreams and follies. Chapter two will more fully explore the modern themes in MacNeice's work. More especially I shall focus on the theme of the self's alienation from the external world resulting from the disrupted harmony with nature brought by industrialisation, but also more deeply sensed because the personal character of each man's perceiving is now recognised, and MacNeice, with the moderns, cannot be sure that any order he may perceive in flux is anything other than his own creation, much as he may wish to find pattern, and so meaning, in the life which seems 'more chances missed than I could count'.

In chapter three, the main argument of this book appears; here I outline the powerful scheme of values in which MacNeice's poetry seems eventually to take root and develop beyond the fragile lyricism or faded urbanity of a frustrated Romantic. In this scheme life in all its variety is valuable because it is the opposite of stasis and death. Together the flux of life and the awful permanence of death create the tension which men need, to stimulate mind, heart and senses to full vigour. The two inseparable opposites of the infinite unchanging One into which all being goes, and the multiple flux of all that now is, seem to MacNeice to give each other value, to co-exist in a metaphysical relation which the poet can accept with bittersweet emotions, and can trust as real. This is a sceptical faith, which believes that no transcendent reality, but rather non-being, gives being value. It rejects religious or Idealistic conceptions without falling into nihilism or despair. Instead of taking up and failing in the Romantic poet's search for an underlying Absolute, MacNeice learns to celebrate

> *The blessedness of fact*
> *Which lives in the dancing atom and the breathing*
> *trees*

even rejoicing that they live briefly, that

> *the value*
> *Of every organism, act and moment*
> *Is, thanks to death, unique.*

In Part II I shall turn my attention to the more technical aspects of MacNeice's verse, first identifying them and then attempting to argue that many of them can be seen as the embodiment of the basic sceptical vision which is the 'centre' of his work, the 'idea' behind his poetic achievement. This argument will assume the position adopted by J. Hillis Miller in his book *Charles Dickens: The World of His Novels* in which he states of literary criticism that it can, through the revelation of 'the persistence of certain obsessions, problems and attitudes', enable the critic 'to glimpse the original unity of a creative mind.' The argument further accepts Miller's dictum :

> The persuasive stylistic traits of a writer, his recurrent words and images, his special cadence and tone of voice, are as personal to him as his face or way of walking . . . A poem or novel is indeed the world refashioned into conformity with the inner structure of the writer's spirit, but at the same time it is that spirit given, through words, a form and substance taken from the shared solidity of the exterior world.

It is crucial to point out of course that this view of literature does not depend upon the writer's awareness of the significance of his techniques. He may employ them for his own good reasons, but their significance may be quite other than that he intended. A man's style is like his clothes, it creates its own meanings often irrespective of intentions. So in arguing for the existence of a relationship between the poet's characteristic techniques and his fundamental view of the world, I am not suggesting that the poet always consciously chose the techniques to embody his outlook (though he was sometimes aware of the relationship), but that style is inevitably a revelation of a man's world-view, as his clothes reveal things about his personality and sense of himself. So, 'through art we can know another's view of the universe'.

I hope it will become clear that the scepticism I can see at the centre of MacNeice's poetry, determining both its form and content, is creative. I feel it is so, since it forces MacNeice to write about certain subjects, to make a certain kind of complex affirmation of the world, and since it drives him to certain technical procedures and strategies, which establish his poetry as unique; it determines his own, recognisable, tones of voice.

This book is an attempt to defend MacNeice from the charge of superficiality, to take him seriously. I trust it will encourage others to read his poetry with more concern for the poet's ideas, forms, and tones of voice, and more awareness of the significance of his achievement.

The Roots of Art

Such and such my beginnings, launched and engined
With such and such a tackle of nerve and gland
And steered by such and such taboos and values,
My What and How science might understand
But neither the first nor last page tells the story
And that I am remains just that I am.
The whole, though predetermined to a comma,
Still keeps its time, its place, its glory.

(*Day of Renewal*)

Louis MacNeice's poetry reveals to its readers a consciousness ordered and controlled by scepticism. This intellectual and emotional reaction to life that the poetry records was not the enervating, destructive thing it might have been for the poet, but a positively creative element in his artistic sensibility. How such a creatively sceptical personality developed is a matter for biographical exploration; its manifestations in art, a matter for criticism. In this chapter I shall concentrate on biography. Criticism will be my concern in later chapters.

Some men seem, like Pallas Athene, to emerge from the face of life fully formed. Nothing of importance appears to have happened to them before adulthood. It is difficult, for example, to imagine Milton as a child; his biography, as his writing, is an affair of state, of the adult dialectitian, of the theological controversialist and innovator. Such men seldom refer directly to their childhoods; they reckon them unimportant and as a result so do we. Other men, however, seem never to escape the memories and constraints of their earliest experiences; their personal concentration on childhood seems no mere Romantic literary affectation but a recurrent need. For all the pressing immediacy of adult experience, the importance of childhood events remains crucial to their self-awareness. Louis MacNeice was one such, exhibiting a life-long preoccupation with his origins. He wrote one long autobiographical fragment, *The Strings are False*, and several articles about his childhood and adolescence, while even some of his literary criticism has an autobiographical framework. Incidents from childhood form the basis of many of his poems, his concern with his past in truth amounting, in Professor Dodds's words, 'almost to an obsession'.[1] In seeking for the roots of MacNeice's apprehension of the world, we would do right, I believe, to focus attention on the poet's childhood and his adult relationship with his past.

Louis MacNeice was born in Belfast in 1907, the third child of the marriage of the Reverend John Frederick MacNeice and Elizabeth Clesham. Shortly after Louis's birth the MacNeices moved to the small Co. Antrim town of Carrickfergus, now a dormitory suburb of the city, then distinctly its own place with a castle, factories and Scots and Irish quarters. It was a coastal town, where the sea, that so occupied the poet's adult imagination, nightly insinuated its way into his sleep in the sounds of ships sailing down Belfast lough (see his poem *Carrickfergus*).

MacNeice spent most of his first years almost exclusively in his mother's company. There seem to have been no other children, apart from his mentally retarded brother and his sister, in the MacNeices' immediate vicinity, with whom he might properly have associated. A notable feature of the early sections of *The Strings are False* is that few other children are mentioned, apart from the family. MacNeice's parents, as Spender's, kept him 'from children who were rough'. His early relationship with his mother must have been especially close, for her sudden departure for hospital and then news of her untimely death had a profoundly unsettling effect upon him. MacNeice's sister has recorded her impressions of her brother's reaction at this time (the early months of 1913):

In March 1913 she had an operation which completely cured her former malady, but at the same time she quite suddenly developed an agitated melancholia. Louis and I saw her change almost overnight from a mother who had always been the mainstay of the household—serene and comforting, apparently the very essence of stability—into someone who was deeply unhappy, and no longer able to make decisions. Louis in particular, as the youngest, was greatly attached to his mother, and before her illness I remember him as being with her a very great deal. She always remained gentle and loving, but as she became more and more sad and restless Louis, who was only five and a half, must have been completely bewildered and greatly disturbed. His last memory-picture of her walking up and down the garden path in tears seems to have haunted him for the rest of his life.[2]

His sister comments: 'I think that the shock of seeing the sudden change in the mother he loved so much, followed by the uncertainty of her return, may have been the chief factor which caused Louis's memories of childhood to be so sad and sometimes so bitter.' This fracturing of experience, this inexplicable rift in a secret childhood world, that MacNeice remembered with poignant regret in his poem *Autobiography*, may partly account for the scepticism of his developed personality. Belief requires a trust in life, a security in the world, even sometimes a complacency, that such events would do much to destroy. Later as a young man MacNeice was to experience an equivalent catastrophe in the collapse of his first marriage, which would increase his insecurity: his first wife walked out on their marriage with an alarming abruptness. The poet writes of this event, in *The Strings are False*, with reticence and controlled economy of detail that powerfully suggest the shock and pain it occasioned him: 'The next morning Mariette left for London, there to join Tsalic and not to come back again . . . the day Mariette left I felt very desolate.'[3] Such an event, I suggest, would do little but confirm a man in any insecurity his childhood may have induced.

Many of MacNeice's friends and acquaintances have left us records of his adult personality. Frequently they remark on a quite extraordinary shyness, a stand-offishness, that some interpreted as superciliousness, arrogance, but others, I feel more accurately, identified as a deep suspiciousness of experience, a wary, self-protective canniness which avoided commitments that might not have proved fully worthwhile. John Hilton, who knew MacNeice well as his contemporary at Marlborough and Oxford, remembers the poet as a young man:

On the whole at that time he preferred to study mankind indirectly. . . . He practised in this way a certain spiritual economy that I take to have been necessary to the protection of his inner world. He was afraid—as in the 'Prayer before birth'—of being spilled. He did not mind at times appearing sly; he did not always choose to recognise people he had met before (though his increasing short-sightedness was probably responsible for many imagined offences of this kind).[4]

Desmond Pacey, who met MacNeice at Cambridge while the poet was giving the Clark Lectures in 1963 (the year of his death) remembers him as a deeply reserved man : 'as a dinner companion MacNeice was serious, reticent and almost inarticulate. His shyness and nervousness revealed themselves by his habit of chain-smoking cigarettes in the Fellows parlour before dinner, and by the obvious impatience with which he waited for the opportunity to smoke after the port in the Senior Combination Room.'[5]

This self-protective reserve bespeaks a fundamental distrust of experience, of relationships, that may well have had its roots in the poet's childhood :

> *When I was five the black dream came;*
> *Nothing after was quite the same.*
> . . . .
> *I got up; the chilly sun*
> *Saw me walk away alone.*
>
> *(Autobiography)*

Insecurity and a resultant inability to make commitments easily, that helped make MacNeice a sceptic, may have been heightened by further complications in the poet's background : Louis MacNeice was, though many of his critics have neglected this fact, an Anglo-Irish exile.

MacNeice's father John Frederick MacNeice was an individual of unusual sympathies and qualities. A Church of Ireland rector in a Northern Irish parish, in 1912 he supported Home Rule for Ireland against much enthusiastic local feeling. This Nationalist stand was counter to what one might have expected of a man of his particular class and creed at that time. The Church of Ireland in 1912 was still deeply involved with the Protestant Ascendancy which had dominated Ireland politically with its wealth and influence since the eighteenth century. Most members of the Church were Unionist in politics and convinced defenders of the *status quo*, deferring to the Ascendancy from whose ranks the Church's governing hierarchy, in the main, derived. As a rector of a Northern parish, later to occupy a bishop's palace, it was extraordinary that MacNeice's father should have developed Nationalist sympathies. By birth, social and educational experience (at Trinity College, Dublin at a period when its outlook was anything but Nationalist) his political views might have been expected to coincide unambiguously with the interests of Anglo-Ireland.

Louis MacNeice once suggested that his childhood was in many respects similar to that of W. B. Yeats: 'When I read Yeats's account of his childhood I find many things which are echoed in my own or in that of other Irish people I know—in particular, the effects of loneliness, or a primitive rural life; the clannish obsession with one's own family . . .'[6]

The similarities that MacNeice remarks are probably related to the fact that both families occupied an anomalous social position in the Ireland of their time. Not all Irish children were solitaries or obsessed with pedigree. Both the poets' fathers were, however, Protestant Nationalists at a time when to be such was an almost certain guarantee of isolation and loneliness. In the turbulent world of late nineteenth- and early twentieth-century Irish politics, a Church of Ireland Protestant who cultivated a sympathy for the separatist aspirations of Catholic Ireland naturally set himself apart from the majority of his co-religionists, while his dedication to the Irish cause fell under the suspiciously sceptical examination of Catholic Nationalists. For Irish Nationalism was not entirely convinced, despite the evidence of a line of Protestant patriots, that a non-Catholic could fully share in the nation's struggle. Indeed when, in 1912, John Frederick MacNeice refused to sign the Ulster Covenant in the name of a peacefully negotiated semi-independence for a country in which every kind of Irishman might feel at home, it was probably the last time that such a stance could have made much political sense. For the next ten years were to see the rise and consolidation in political structures, of two militant and mutually exclusive versions of Irish identity, the Catholic Gaelic and the Orange Unionist.

For all those associated with Anglo-Ireland in any way, the period (which was that of Louis MacNeice's childhood and adolescence) was one of profound identity crisis. Anglican and propertied, Anglo-Ireland recoiled from the non-conformist populism of Ulster's vocal 'loyalty' but its members found themselves confronted in the rest of Ireland, whether they had Nationalist sympathies or not, with a conception of Irish identity which excluded Protestants from full spiritual citizenship in the Irish nation. Stephen Gwynn, an Ascendancy Nationalist who had hoped for a negotiated settlement to the Irish Question, wrote of his awakening identity crisis in this period : 'I was brought up to think myself Irish, without question or qualification; but the new nationalism prefers to describe me and the like of, as Anglo-Irish. A.E. has even set me down in print as being . . . the typical Anglo-Irishman. So all my life I have been spiritually hyphenated without knowing it.'[7]

There were many signs of spiritual hyphenation in the MacNeice household. Louis's father was clearly unhappy in loyalist Ulster, frequently nostalgic for the Connemara of his earliest days. But despite his love for the West of Ireland, the activities of the Republican movement there so distressed him that he forwent visits across the newly established border, for a time : 'In a later September (for my seventeenth birthday) we went to Donegal, my first holiday in the "South". . . . We should have gone south earlier had it not been for the Troubles; my father, in spite of his nationalism, had said, "How can you mix with people who might be murderers without you knowing it?" '[8]

On a holiday visit to Scotland MacNeice's father was at pains to compare 'his own countrymen unfavourably with the hard-working, well-informed, clean and thrifty Scots'.[9] MacNeice assumed that Trinity College, Dublin was ruled out for him as a possible university when he left Marlborough 'because of the doings in that city'.[10] Dublin was, however, 'a glorious name' in the family and his father obviously had a deep love for the Irish landscape and for Ireland's people, apart, occasionally, from their politics. MacNeice in *The Strings are False* describes him visiting the West of Ireland, exulting in a first glimpse of the sea, exploring the graves of his ancestors, remembering tales he had been told as a child on the island of Omey : 'My father was remembering the stories the fishermen used to tell him about the houses and the towers were down under the sea, and he was looking around for the rookeries all the rooks had left, and his nostalgia would make him walk fast, swinging his stick, and then break off impatiently. "Terribly backward" he would say, "terribly backward".[11] In such a moment is caught all the strained ambivalence of feeling experienced by an Anglo-Irishman of Nationalist sympathies in the 1920s. His reaction is a blend of dismay and ineradicable love.

Born to a class and creed whose members were under great social and political pressure Louis MacNeice inevitably felt certain strains. From earliest days he experienced the tension of conflicting loyalties that his position as son of a Nationalist rector in the North of Ireland involved. Ulster to the child's imagination was a region of encroaching Calvinist religion, grim drums of the Orange faction and the fierce children of the Catholic poor. In his solitary life in the large rectory and garden (which entered deeply into his imagination) he hankered for Connemara and the West of Ireland, which as yet he had not visited. Sensing his father's preference for the South of Ireland he developed a taste for rebel songs as the young Yeats before him had expressed his childish alienation from the world of the Dublin middle classes by defiant renditions of Orange ballads.

School in England (at Sherborne) soon became preferable to the loneliness and tension of home, but the tensions could not be escaped entirely. He quickly found playing the 'wild Irish boy' a suitable ruse to gain popularity. But Irishness obtruded at embarrassing moments :

On the Twelfth of July Powys came into my dormitory and said : 'What is all this they do in your country to-day? Isn't it all mumbo-jumbo?' Remembering my father and Home Rule and the bony elbows of Miss Craig and the black file of mill-girls and the wickedness of Carson and the dull dank days between sodden haycocks and foghorns, I said Yes it was. And I felt uplifted. To be speaking man to man to Powys and giving the lie to the Red Hand of Ulster, was power, was freedom, meant I was nearly grown up. King William was dead and his white horse with him . . . That the Twelfth of July was mumbo-jumbo was true, and my father thought so too,

B

but the moment Mr Cameron appeared I felt rather guilty and cheap. Because I had been showing off to Powys and because Mr. Cameron being after all Irish I felt I had betrayed him.[12]

Such insecurity as this incident betrays (and MacNeice recounts others in *The Strings are False*) would develop in adulthood into the poet's persistent inability to solve the problem of his nationality and into the complex of unresolved attitudes that represented his response to it. For the Ireland that emerged in the first decades of Louis MacNeice's life, that had placed his father's world in jeopardy, would never command the poet's uncomplicated loyalty. As an adult MacNeice, educated abroad and domiciled in England, would find himself alienated from both versions of Irish identity that had so violently asserted themselves in his lifetime. He would castigate Orange and Green with equal bitterness in a long painfully angry section of his poem *Autumn Journal* (1938). Proudly convinced from childhood of his own ancestry as a marriage of Celtic peasant strength and aristocratic style, denying that mere planters' blood, such as that which flowed so unattractively in Orange veins, had corrupted his Irish inheritance, he nevertheless would have little enthusiasm for the State the native Irish developed in the first modern period of political independence. For in a number of poems (*Valediction* and *Autumn Journal* in particular) which are a tense blend of pained affection and satiric repugnance he would anatomise the country. Ireland's *penchant* for dangerous fantasy, for myopic myth, for political and cultural befuddlement, for human waste in the cause of unrealistic abstraction, would be surgically analysed in his poems, until a near total disillusionment resulted from Ireland's neutrality in the Second World War when in *Neutrality* he would write a savage indictment of what he saw as the country's callous self-absorption at a time of international crisis.

Yet MacNeice for all his disillusion with his native country could never manage to break with it. He remained to his death an exile rather than an ex-patriot, unable to sever all links with Ireland. In 1939 he applied for the Chair of English at Trinity College, Dublin, but was not successful (as Yeats had not been when he too sought appointment to the Chair at an earlier period). In 1940 shortly after the death of W. B. Yeats (who had taken an interest in MacNeice's career) the Cuala press brought out a volume of MacNeice's poems (*The Last Ditch*) signalling that the Yeats family shared the older poet's estimation of the younger. MacNeice was also for a time the poetry editor of the remarkable Irish periodical *The Bell* (edited in Dublin by the distinguished Irish short-story writer Sean O'Faolain) which was one of the few public organs in the monolithic cultural conservatism of 1940s Ireland in which the kind of criticisms that MacNeice made of the country would have had any chance of sympathetic consideration.

Unable to settle in Ireland, MacNeice did not become, at any stage in his career, fully integrated into English society despite the fact that England was his chosen country of residence and the country that gave him his livelihood. The English tended to think of him as Irish; critics referred to his nationality when they reviewed his books. He was called upon to deliver his opinion on Irish matters from time to time. The *New Statesman,* for instance, sent him as a correspondent to cover Irish events (he reported on President Kennedy's visit to Ireland in 1962 in its columns), and frequently used him as a reviewer of books of Irish interest. But in Belfast and Dublin his nationality was more in question. In the North of Ireland his English education and his English voice were often noticed by the provincially sensitive. Ulster does not readily welcome those of its sons who appear to affect an English accent and whose families spurn what it believes to be adequate local educational facilities. As sympathetic a critic as the Ulster poet Roy McFadden once censured MacNeice for his lack of regionalistic loyalty :

> The only uneasy ghost in Mr. MacNeice's mind is his place of origin. From time to time the poet reverts to Ireland, nostalgically, impatiently, contemptuously—only to set his face firmly again towards the English scene. This retreat from childhood and country is a pity, for in the absence of any spiritual roots Mr. MacNeice might have strengthened his work by allegiance to place.[13]

Other Ulstermen might not have put such a polite word upon it. In Dublin, his criticisms of the new Ireland, truthful as they may have been, were hardly likely to have won him many friends.

And the Dublin literary world, notoriously introspective, sometimes even narcissistic, considered the poet who worked and published in London and who criticised Ireland outspokenly, as Irish in no important sense. The city that rejected Synge, Joyce and O'Casey did not give Louis MacNeice a particularly warm reception. MacNeice loved Dublin, where he felt 'at home . . . more than in any other city';[14] he wrote one of the finest poetic evocations of that city that I know (*Dublin*). But in Dublin he has always been thought of as an outsider; a jingle he himself reports sums up the prevailing attitude :

> *Let him go back and labour*
> *For Faber and Faber.*

As he regretfully admitted :

> *This was never my town,*
> *I was not born and bred*
> *Nor schooled here and she will not*
> *Have me alive or dead . . .*
> (*The Closing Album: Dublin*)

MacNeice never resolved the tensions in which his position as Anglo-Irish exile involved him. In the last years of his life he and a fellow Ulster poet, W. R. Rodgers, were commissioned to edit a book about Ireland for the Clarendon Press. The work never appeared, though the poem MacNeice wrote for its prologue was published in *The Listener* in 1971. The poem evokes the jumble of opposites that Ireland represented in MacNeice's imagination, but does not achieve an actual synthesis, though gesturing towards such. Living in a painful no-man's land between Ireland and England, suffering from the effects of the spiritual hyphenation, the complex of conflicting loyalties, which were the common property of Irishmen of his class and social experience in the first half of this century, the problem was probably not soluble in any simple way.

> *Torn before birth from where my fathers dwelt,*
> *Schooled from the age of ten to a foreign voice,*
> *Yet neither western Ireland nor southern England*
> *Cancels this interlude; what chance misspelt*
> *May never now be righted by my choice.*

Whatever then my inherited or acquired
Affinities, such remains my childhood's frame
Like a belated rock in the red Antrim clay
That cannot at this era change its pitch or name—
And the pre-natal mountain is far away.
                              (Carrick Revisited)

He was the true exile. He spent time in various countries, in
America, where he went on a number of lecture tours, Greece
where he served in Athens with the British Council for a period
of eighteen months (1950-51), in South Africa where he lectured
at the University of Cape Town, and in India and Pakistan, but
in none does he seem to have been moved to anything beyond the
intelligent tourist's response. Where other writers of MacNeice's
generation sought out cultures and locations with which they
might identify, MacNeice remained detached. Isherwood after
his period in Berlin would happily settle in the sunshine of
California, Auden would opt for American citizenship and the
life of a New Yorker, but for MacNeice, exile from Ireland left
him, finally, a stranger everywhere.

A personality so early confronted by the knowledge of life's
impermanence and assailed throughout life by conflicting social
and cultural loyalties would obviously not be one to whom belief
and commitment would come easily. To MacNeice childhood
and young adulthood brought bereavement and loss. The
accidents of history cast him in the perplexing role of
Anglo-Irish exile. That his personality as we encounter it in his
poetry should bear the stamp of a settled scepticism does not
surprise.

Had the ambience of an English upper-middle class education
in the 1920s been different, however, MacNeice's developing
personality might have met a challenge, both intellectual and
emotional, that could have redirected it towards belief. In fact
MacNeice's experiences at public school and University (Marlborough and Merton College, Oxford), together with the general
atmosphere of the times, did little but confirm the poet's predilection for unresolved disbelief. Michael Roberts, who was to
espouse Marxism in the thirties, to edit two famous anthologies of
left-wing verse (*New Signatures* and *New Country*) and eventually to join the Church of England, has recorded his impressions

of the contemporary mood among the educated young in the twenties :

> Those of us who grew up to manhood in the post-war years remember how, in that period, it seemed to us there was no finality. We learned to question every impulse until we became so self-conscious, so hag-ridden by doubts, indecisions, uncertainties that we lost all spontaneity, and, because we learned to account for the actions of others, we learned neither to praise nor blame them. It was not any one thing which caused this scepticism : it appeared in various guises—the theory of relativity breaking up our neat mechanical world, science learning to doubt whether it could approach any finality, psychoanalysis discovering how many actions, apparently spontaneous, were rigidly determined; and beyond all this a feeling that the middle-class world, the world of the nineteenth century, was definitely breaking up, and that it would be replaced in the near future by a world of communism or big business.[15]

As an adolescent MacNeice read with enthusiastic eclecticism. He was fortunate to be at Marlborough with an extraordinarily precocious group of contemporaries which included Anthony Blunt and John Betjeman. Their tastes in art and literature ranged from the ostentatiously avant-garde to the cultivatedly whimsical. Cezanne, Matisse, Aldous Huxley, T. S. Eliot, Lord Dunsany's fairy tales, Edward Lear's nonsense rhymes, helped form their personal Pantheon. To these MacNeice added Greek philosophy (particularly Heraclitus) and his own 'sacred books', *Prometheus Unbound, The Golden Ass* of Apuleius, Dasent's translation of *Burnt Njal,* and *Morte d'Arthur*. It was a heady world as MacNeice paints it in *The Strings are False,* remote from the rectory in County Antrim. The schoolmaster whom MacNeice most admired at Marlborough was G. M. Sargeaunt who 'had a private religion of his own founded on ancient Stoicism', which must have provided him with a sense of exhilarating release from the oppressive Christian orthodoxies of his native Ulster. After Marlborough, even Oxford proved something of a disappointment ('Oxford seemed hardly to have heard of the Post-Impressionists')[16] while his visits home were difficult occasions. For it must not be forgotten how great a gulf there was between MacNeice's home and such a world of exciting discovery. At home was the family's serious, almost Victorian conviction of religion's and morality's importance; at school 'the only real values were aesthetic. Moral values were a delusion and politics a waste of time.'[17] In such an atmosphere MacNeice's personality, already prepared for scepticism, would have met little to prevent its settling in a sceptical mould as he became a particularly precocious and intelligent member of a generation to whom 'it seemed there was no finality'.

Many of MacNeice's generation were, as we shall see, soon to follow Michael Roberts's path, sinking their doubts for a time in the Marxism they enthusiastically discovered in the 1930s. MacNeice, while others joined the Communist Party or wrote stirring calls to Socialist action, was to maintain a position of slightly disdainful scepticism. The roots of his scepticism were, it seems, deeper and more personal than they were for some of his contemporaries, who when the *Zeitgeist* was for cynical or pessimistic disbelief were doubters and, when for Marxism, rather simple-minded acolytes of that demandingly optimistic ideology. MacNeice's scepticism, formed in childhood and early manhood by a series of personal catastrophes and historic accidents, which met little resistance and much confirmation in his education at Marlborough and Oxford, was by the thirties too settled an element in his make-up to allow for any simplistic commitment to a teleology of history, or to a promised future of social bliss.[18]

As an adult Louis MacNeice, so much a product of conflicting influences and personal tensions, might well have become a cynic or a despairing nihilist. With little to hold on to by way of creed or country, little to grasp as permanent in a world of personal and social change, the temptation simply to drift with events, snatching such transitory alleviations of the pains of life as an epicurean sensualism or hedonistic self-regard might provide, must have indeed been powerful. How MacNeice strenuously avoided succumbing to such temptations, staving off both cynicism and despair will be a matter for later chapters. Why he should have felt and thought himself obliged to avoid them is my immediate concern.

MacNeice's father John Frederick MacNeice was not a man who would have admired any cynical or despairing view of life. Firmly convinced of the truth of the Christian religion his years of service in the Church of Ireland are a record of earnest commitment, energy and vision. Born the son of a rural school-master, in the West of Ireland, he was to receive his education at Trinity College, Dublin (graduating with academic honours in 1895), to be ordained into the Church in which he would be consecrated bishop of a Northern Irish see at a time of great social and political import. He was a man of broad sympathies; he was intelligent, courageous, outspoken, and he was a puritan. His nationalistic feeling for Ireland was no narrow chauvinism or intolerant xenophobia, but a matter of fundamental concern for all the inhabitants of the island. His own father had expressed concern for the Irish people by serving for a number of years as a member of an Anglican missionary society, and John Frederick MacNeice clearly inherited an evangelistic urge. But he coupled it with a keen intelligence. His Nationalism was therefore co-herently intellectual as well as deeply felt. A passage from his monograph *Carrickfergus and its Contacts* reveals the cast of his mind :

> Possibly there has been nothing so magnificent in political his-tory as England's work in India. To this country she sent her wisest, ablest administrators. The problem to be solved was studied with the utmost diligence. But in Ireland, England's record has been different. The history of English rule in Ireland is, in large measure, the history of opportunities that were missed, of want of vision, want of sympathy, want of capacity on the part of those who were entrusted with the government of the country. Third and fourth rate politicians were appointed Viceroys and Chief Secretaries. They were ignorant when they came and as ignorant when they departed. There were of course exceptions. Now and again a man of first-class brains was sent to Ireland but as he did not stay long his presence made little permanent difference.[19]

Such fair-minded, astringent analysis of the Irish situation did not often come from Protestant clergymen in the Ireland of 1928.

He had the courage of his convictions too, for in the midst of political hysteria in 1912 he preached a brave sermon from his Carrickfergus pulpit counselling restraint, arguing against those of his countrymen who swore to take up arms to defend the Union of Ireland with Great Britain 'that even the avowal of such a policy may add to the dissensions that are already too

characteristic of Irish life, and intensify the bitterness that many
. . . hoped was fast dying away.'[20] He recorded later with dignified reserve that such thinking 'represented a minority, negligible
indeed in numbers, whose conscientious scruples exposed them at
the time to some adverse criticism.'[21] One imagines that they
did.

John Frederick MacNeice linked his Nationalism to a genuine,
believing Christianity. Although he did not lack worldly wisdom,
his published work, his letters to the press, and his recorded
sermons, reveal a man convinced of the Church's role as a peace-
maker in society and of petitionary prayer as a vital and necessary reality in a nation's life. In 1920 he, and a group of
Carrickfergus ministers of religion, wrote to the Irish press suggesting the establishment of a League of Prayer for Ireland, as a
response to the political and civil crises of that year. The tone is
of a strong-minded, Christian commitment and urgency:

> The situation in Ireland is becoming more and more alarming
> daily: the country seems to be moving towards utter anarchy.
> . . . What happened in Derry may happen elsewhere if action
> by those who believe in Christ, and who in a special sense
> are His representatives in Ireland, is delayed much longer. The
> people of Derry are all members of Christian churches. . . .
> If the Christian forces were only mobilised in time there could
> be no serious rioting in Derry or elsewhere.[22]

John Frederick MacNeice's faith, as his Nationalism, was
humane and broadly conceived (in 1929 he preached a sermon
in Trinity College, Dublin encouraging Irish ecumenism, and
published a study of Inter-Church developments in South India
—each remarkable statements for their period) but it was firm
and unshakeable. The same qualities of direct strong-mindedness
and blunt honesty that he brought to his political utterances
(he, although a Nationalist, castigated the Home Rule leaders
for their ignorance of Protestant Ulster—'a very tragic and stupid
mistake') allowed him to cut through the sectarian self-interest
of the Irish Churches with a controlled eloquence that established
his position as a very remarkable Irish churchman indeed.

The streak of puritanism in his personality, which must have
rendered him, a Nationalist sympathiser from the South, more
acceptable to his Ulster congregations, revealed itself in his strict

teetotal stand, while the high degree of responsibility that he brought to duties in the Church and the seriousness with which he fulfilled them, were undoubtedly effects of his puritan sense of life. The world for Bishop MacNeice, as is quickly evident from his published sermons, was a place for effort, enthusiasm, and intelligent commitment, while religion was as much a part of his life as eating and sleeping : 'Religion never left us alone, it was at home as much as in church, it fluttered in the pages of a tear-off calendar in the bathroom and it filled the kitchen with the smell of silver polish when Annie, who might at the same time be making jokes about John Jameson, was cleaning the communion plate.'[23] John Hilton, a contemporary of Louis's at Marlborough and Oxford who visited his home in Ireland, recalls the man : 'There was a quiet, rugged grandeur about Archdeacon, later Bishop, MacNeice which could not fail to communicate itself; . . . against the setting of the slums of Belfast and all the troubles of Ireland. . . .'[24]

To be the son of such a father would be difficult even if one shared his faith. To break with his Church and creed would be a serious matter. For MacNeice it must have been as painful an experience as it was for Matthew Arnold to deny his parent's vigorous Christianity. Indeed MacNeice's home background was probably more akin to that of the Victorian poet's than it was to that of many of his English contemporaries. His ostentatiously modern poetic surfaces, especially in his early poetry, should not disguise the fact that the source of his personality lay far from the world of arterial roads, Freud and Marx, T.V., airports, contraceptives, the H-bomb and supermarkets, in a County Antrim rectory that in the Ireland of the first decades of the century would have been much closer in atmosphere and fundamental assumptions to those of a conservatively religious Victorian home than to anything we might recognise as twentieth-century English middle-class. In a brief voyage across the Irish sea MacNeice left one era for another.

As a child MacNeice was in considerable awe of his most impressive father : 'My mother was comfort and my father somewhat alarm.' He was afraid of his father's 'conspiracy with God' and of his father's black nights after his first wife's death : 'I now slept in his room and found it even worse than the nightmares. Because he was sleeping very badly, [he] would toss and groan through the night, so that, if I was awake when he came up, I would be kept awake for hours listening to him; but always pretended to be asleep. My great objective now was really to be asleep before he arrived with the lamp and his own gigantic shadow.'[25]

At Oxford MacNeice, with what appears to have been a degree of deliberation, precipitated a clash with his background and his father when he took vigorously to alcohol (he spent a night in a local police-station after one bacchanalia) and suddenly announced his engagement to a Jewish girl. But his rebellion was by no means untroubled. At school he had feared the loss of his faith as he felt it slipping from him. He had been troubled by dreams, one of them particularly expressive of his ambivalent feelings at the time :

> One night, lying in the great green dormitory, I found myself walking with my father over the downs. We were ascending a slope that was cut off blind by the sky and I was walking some way ahead. As I came near the skyline there was the noise of a funfair and a tall scarlet soldier standing stiff in a bearskin, woodenly abstracted. I reached his level, topping the curve of the world, the brass music blared up full and down below me was Calvary. Not on a hill—that was the first correction—but far down below me in an amphitheatre cut in the chalk. Tiers and tiers of people in gala dress—bunting, rattles and paper streamers—and in the arena were the three bodies on the crosses. A sight to make you retch and I knew if my father saw it all would be over. He was drawing up behind me when I woke.[26]

This disturbingly graphic vision of Christ and the world (perhaps the fairground is a recreation of Vanity Fair in Bunyan's *Pilgrim's Progress*—a work MacNeice surely encountered in his rectory childhood) reveals how deeply the figure of his father had penetrated his imagination. Nor is the dream likely to have come to one lightly casting aside his Christian inheritance. In a passage in *Autumn Sequel* (published in 1954) MacNeice was to assess this vision as 'the worst of my dreams', recognising it as the moment in which he realised the reality of his own doubt and of his father's faith. At Oxford MacNeice cultivated a stance of deliberate condescension towards religious belief (William

James's *Varieties of Religious Experience* confirmed his dis-
affiliation) declaring, especially if a clergyman was within earshot,
with a typically undergraduate iconoclasm 'that religion was
nonsense'. Yet the 'ikons' retained something of their power
(as they were to do throughout the poet's life) :

> Even as I would say this, I would feel rather hypocritical, for,
> greatly though he now exasperated me, I would remember
> how my father would come in to breakfast on Easter Day
> beaming as though he had just received a legacy; and I realised
> that his life, though not by any stretch of the imagination a life
> for me, was more all of a piece, more purposeful, more satis-
> factory to himself and perhaps to others than the lives of most
> people I knew.[27]

As a poet MacNeice was to turn again and again to the figure
of his father and the images of his Church. The clash of youth,
as time passed, developed into something more mellow. In fact
MacNeice's poems on his father reveal the same almost grudging
regard that the above admission records. In adult life, in exile
from both country and creed, MacNeice seems to have seen in
his father an ideal of Irish Christianity that he admired but
could not embrace. Stern, strong, consistent, meaningfully integrated with its environment, it demanded respect :

> *A square black figure whom the horizon understood—*
> *My father.*
>
> > (*The Strand*)

It was this figure and the poet's sense of its stature, that, I
feel sure, accounts for MacNeice's refusal to dissipate his personality in cynicism or despair. In both fearing and finally admiring a father whose life so clearly exemplified the virtues of
responsibility and duty, social commitment and faith-induced
purpose, the poet's sceptical sensibility had a counter-balance
to those forces that drew it towards life denial.

MacNeice's sense of duty quickly revealed itself after a period
of cocooned aestheticism at Oxford. Teaching Classics at Birmingham University (he had graduated with a first class degree
in the subject) in the years of the economic depression he began
to be aware (especially after Mariette's departure) of the lot of the
majority of his fellow creatures. One day the ashplant that he had

carried in affected imitation of Stephen Dedalus since his Oxford days got left behind him in a pub while he went out for a walk with an electrician. His re-education was complete. From this point on, his natural human sympathy began to receive freer expression. He began to make friends with a much wider spectrum of human type than he had hitherto. His interest in and feeling for ordinary social experience began to develop as his aesthete's mandarinism gave way to a democratic openness that allowed him to become acquainted with individuals outside the world of public schools, Oxbridge and Academe. Indeed one of the most notable features of MacNeice's mature personality as we meet it in his writings and the records of his friends is the degree to which he seems to have shared the tastes and evaluations of the non-literary as well as those of the literary. His interests were wide-ranging—books, films, sport, talk, popular songs, gardening, flowers, animals. Rugby football remained one of his passions, while he admired and was friendly with men of action—soldiers, sportsmen, business men—all his life. When, in Birmingham, he allowed himself to shake off the values of cultivated aestheticism that aspects of his education had imparted to him, his sense of identity with common life, that he probably inherited from his father (who for all his impressiveness had a streak of boyish, naïve enthusiasm in his personality) reasserted itself, to set him apart from many of his literary peers who, with the exception of his school-fellow John Betjeman and perhaps of W. H. Auden, had little non-ironic fellow-feeling for the life of suburban and working-class man. It is difficult in fact to think of a poet of MacNeice's generation to whom his own description of the ideal poetic personality might apply, apart from MacNeice himself:

> My own prejudice, therefore, is in favour of poets whose worlds are not too esoteric. I would have a poet able-bodied, fond of talking, a reader of the newspapers, capable of pity and laughter, informed in economics, appreciative of women, involved in personal relationships, actively interested in politics, susceptible to physical impressions.[28]

There was a thrust towards the central concerns of the ordinarily human in MacNeice's own sensibility, for all his involvement with the metaphysical problems this book traces, that allowed him closer ties with the mainstreams of contemporary experience than was the case with many other modern poets, who have, in the main, felt themselves on the periphery of life. Almost no poet but MacNeice could have written for instance a poem in praise of shove ha'penny and other pub games (*Indoor Sports*) without irony. MacNeice brought to his poetry a worldly curiosity and a belief in common worldly duty, that has even misled some critics into believing that he was too worldly to be really wise.

In the thirties MacNeice's developing awareness of social issues and of the lives of people outside his own charmed circle of privileged, witty, successful acquaintances soon began to express itself in a desire to write poems that would command a wide readership. He determined to write a poetry that, eschewing estericism, elitism and the need for intensive explication of arcane reference as in Yeats, Pound and Eliot, could appeal to what he defined in his manifesto-like essay of 1938, *Modern Poetry: a Personal Essay,* as an audience of educated ordinary men. If the father had a duty and a role so must the son have; MacNeice's early critical essays are notable for their tone of engaged concern to find that role. And if the poet's thirties commitment to poetry's social function, conceived in almost Wordsworthian terms, became less often and less explicitly expressed as he grew older, his actions and attitudes as a man are consistent with my portrait of a poet to whom responsibility and duty in the world of ordinary men were important virtues. In 1941, despite the opportunity to remain in New York, teaching at Cornell University, and the possibility of marriage to an American girl (she felt unable to leave the United States for the rigours of war-time England) he returned to London, where he volunteered for the Navy (poor health following on a serious operation in the United States ruled him out) served as a fire watcher in the Blitz and gave valuable service in the B.B.C. His twenty-year stint in the features department of that organisation can be seen indeed as a practical extension of his early aspiration to be an artist communicating with a large public. Many of his radio plays and features were, it could be argued, finer examples of the kind of relationship between writer and audience that MacNeice hoped for in the thirties, than some of the poems he wrote at that time. They combine at their best, as in the justly famous *The Dark Tower,* a simplicity of language and structure with a thematic seriousness and tonal astringency. They inform without condescension and entertain without superficiality.

The poet fulfilled his normal social obligations with honesty and care. To the literary work he undertook to supplement his livelihood he gave hard-working attention (his book *Astrology* for instance was more than the coffee-table production it might have been, being a well-researched, interesting volume). He wrote, as well as his poetry and translations, a large amount of occasional literary journalism and some very useful literary criticism. To this work he brought a clear, bracing prose style; avoiding the technical jargon that renders so much academic writing about literature opaque to the general reader, he managed to convey in his criticism a sense of the importance of literature's role as an agent of general culture, without any heavily overt moral tone. He wrote of books so that he could be understood and with an engaging no-nonsense enthusiasm.

Many of MacNeice's friends and acquaintances have borne testimony to his personal trustworthiness and sense of responsibility; it must have seemed oddly appropriate to them that he should have contracted his final illness as a result of his determination to go underground with a recording team to superintend sound-effects for his last radio play (*Persons from Porlock*), when he need not have done so. MacNeice, his close friends tells us, was when he trusted the company, and particularly when drink had thawed the thick ice of his shyness, an engaging, brilliantly witty talker, a marvellously sociable companion. There was however a definite streak of his father's conscientious puritanism in his makeup, related to his taste for physical discomfort and energetic exertion.

To such a man cynicism and despair would always be liable to fall under the interdict of his own inherited and developed sense of responsibility. Despite periods of intense depression, which he attempted to alleviate with alcohol, scepticism could not resign itself to either, nor to a simple hedonism. Throughout his career in fact MacNeice had a sense of duty, not only in respect of his work, friends and social contracts, but to belief itself, rarely underestimating its importance. In *Modern Poetry* he asserted that 'The good poet had a definite attitude to life; most good poets, I fancy, have more than that—they have beliefs (though their beliefs may not be explicit in their work)'.[29]

In his study of W. B. Yeats he turned to the critical problem of the function of belief in poetry, clearly concerned to discover how beliefs as unfashionable and unlikely as the elder poet's related to his undoubted achievement. Here his attempt to solve this critical conundrum (which has perplexed many modern critics) depended on a notion of a coherence between the poet's personality and his beliefs :

> Poets of my generation, who distrust *a priori* methods, tend to found—or to think they found—their own beliefs and their own moral principles on evidence. These beliefs and principles are, in their opinion, of the utmost importance to their poetry. So they are, but not necessarily because they are the 'right' beliefs. Poetry gains body from belief, and the more suited the belief is to the poet, the healthier his poetry; one poet can thrive on pantheism and another on Christianity . . .[30]

It was related coherence between belief and life that MacNeice especially admired in his father, despite his own lack of Christian faith :

> *All is well with*
> *One who believed and practised and whose life*
> *Presumed the Resurrection. What that means*
> *He may have felt he knew; this much is certain—*
> *The meaning filled his actions, made him courteous*
> *And lyrical and strong and kind and truthful,*
> *A generous puritan. . . .*
>
> *(The Kingdom)*

For MacNeice himself, however, beliefs could never be fashioned against the evidence of his own experience. He realised that Yeats had 'misrepresented facts in order to square them with his belief'[31] and had perhaps even 'faked his beliefs because he so much *wanted to believe* . . .'[32] but for him 'any belief and creed . . . should be compromised with individual observation'.[33]

MacNeice, dominated by a sense of impermanence and by cultural tensions, could not have accepted beliefs that would have denied these. Equally his mind could not deny the need for belief, in life and in art. A developed sense of duty, perhaps even of guilt, would also have forbidden a retreat into a despairing nihilism. So I will argue in this book that MacNeice's

poetry is not without its underlying system of values. But the
system he could achieve would clearly not have been one that
would have conflicted with the poet's fundamental scepticism. It
is, rather, a hierarchy of values rooted in and developing from his
sceptical consciousness of the world. His sceptical sensibility,
profoundly aware of the facts of flux, impermanence, death,
established for itself (sometimes quite consciously, sometimes
unconsciously) a coherent view which emerged from his appre-
hensions of these things' ineluctable reality. As I shall argue, it
was from his scepticism that his most complex apprehension—
that of life as a tension between opposites—derived. This sense
was for MacNeice the energising and disciplining force which
allowed him to do justice to his urge to obligation, without in-
justice to 'individual observation'.

Belief, of course, as a constituent of a personality, as one
of the determinants of personal consciousness and vision, is not
necessarily a fully self-conscious thing. A man can, for instance,
order and perceive the world according to humanistic principles,
without knowing himself a humanist or claiming to be one.
When he finally becomes conscious of his adherence to humanistic
values this may simply be the rational mind's reflection on what
has hitherto been a fundamental assumption of the whole man,
feeling and thinking in vital synthesis. MacNeice in his study
of Yeats was at pains to make this point about belief in its
relation to the self of the poet :

> Every poet does two things, though he may be more conscious
> of one than the other and though his success may be due
> more to one than to the other. He reacts emotionally (though
> emotion may be strong or weak, conscious or unconscious)
> to his subject matter and he selects and arranges that subject
> matter—consciously or unconsciously—in order to square it
> with some intellectual system of his own. But even this distinc-
> tion is too crude, for these two moments of the poetic activity
> are inseparable like the positive and negative elements in
> electricity. Even before the artist has started his art work
> proper he is not only reacting emotionally to his subject but
> he is also automatically systematising it.[34]

For MacNeice this 'system', which in the ongoing movement of
life resulted in a process of intellectual and emotional synthesis
c

in poetry, was his sense of life as dialetical tension. This apprehension had been a settled one with the poet. Writing of his childhood he remembers how 'Pleasure was bright and terror had jagged edges'[35] and in the early pages of *The Strings are False* he establishes in retrospection a world where his childish self was afraid of the dark, the violence of sectarian voices, the imagery of the primitive religion he encountered in the nursery, the stone images of his father's church and the bleak tolling of its bell :

> Our life was bounded by this hedge; a granite obelisk would look over it here, and there across the fields of corncrakes could be seen a Norman castle . . . The human elements of this world need not be detailed; guilt, hell fire, Good Friday, the doctor's cough, hurried lamps in the night, melancholia, mongolism, violent sectarian voices. All this sadness and conflict and attrition and frustration were set in this one acre near the smoky town within the sound not only of the tolling bell, but of the smithy that seemed to defy it.[36]

Other things, as well as the bright flames and sparks of the smithy, that defied this world of fixedly oppressive gloom, were the child's imaginary worlds of fairy tales, the West of Ireland, and the bright colours of pleasurable sense-impressions : 'That Christmas we got a great many presents; they were marshalled on the nursery hearthrug by the crackling of the early morning fire. Everything was gay with colour, there were coloured chalks and coloured wooden rattles and striped tin trumpets and tangerines in silver paper, and a copy of *Arabian Nights* with princesses in curly shoes and blue-black hair.'[37]

In his Irish childhood the coordinates of the poet's imagination were marked out. The contradictions and strains of this world, its extremes of darkness and light were to influence how he eventually saw all of life.

The woven figure cannot undo its thread.

(*Valediction*)

PART I

Themes and Attitudes

This man with the shy smile has left behind
Something that was intact.

(*The Suicide*)

I

Misunderstood Romantic

THE scepticism which underlay Louis MacNeice's poetic sensibility, the sensibility of one

> *brought up to scoff rather than to bless*
> *And to say No, unless the facts require . . .*

was not the easy scepticism of a man who has no need of creed.
The fundamental question he poses in *Autumn Journal*:

> *And when we clear away*
> *All this debris of day-to-day experience*
> *What comes out to light, what is there of value*
> *Lasting from day to day?*

is not one that pleases him. His scepticism is that of a poet who
recognises his own hunger, who knows that without beliefs a man
can starve artistically. Had the times been less refractory Mac-
Neice might have sought a faith within the neo-religious, non-
dogmatic attitudes of Romanticism.[1] For the sympathy is there :
Romantic postures, Romantic longing, nostalgia and its imagery
are a constant element throughout his poetry. MacNeice
himself acknowledged that 'whether we like it or not,
an English writer of the twentieth century must have much
more of Shelley in him than of Spenser, say, or Herbert or
Bunyan.'[2]

A characteristic poem from MacNeice's middle years certainly
displays his Romantic predilections. With rhythms of hypnotic
effect in *Western Landscape* MacNeice apostrophises the Western
reaches of both landscape and experience. It is a hymn to
imaginative possibilities with an implied scepticism of attainment
in its emotional tone :

> *O grail of emerald passing light*
> *And hanging smell of sweetest hay*
> *And grain of sea and loom of wind*
> *Weavingly laughingly leavingly weepingly—*
> . . . .
> *O relevance of cloud and rock—*
> *If such could be our permanence!*

Attainment itself is then embodied for the poet in the mythical figure of St Brandan who following his desire into the West, found purpose in continual pursuit of vision, achieving thereby that for which the poet can only long.

> *And yet he bobs beyond that next high crest for ever.*
> . . . .
> *And the West was all the world, the lonely was the only,*
> *The chosen—and there was no choice—the Best,*
> *For the beyond was here . . .*
> *But for us now*
> *The beyond is still out there as on tiptoes here we stand*
> *On promontories that are themselves a-tiptoe*
> *Reluctant to be land.*

This characteristic Romantic stance, reminiscent of Coleridge facing the rising tide of human liberty from a promontory (in *France: An Ode*) or of Keats's famous mariners silent upon their peak in Darien, recurs in a late poem *Donegal Triptych* where communion with solitude, as in Coleridge's conversation poems, provides the poet with solace, paradoxically reminding of common humanity :

> *Once more having entered solitude once more to find*
> *communion*
> *With other solitary beings, with the whole race of men.*

So an uncompromisingly political poem such as *An Eclogue for Christmas* concludes with an escapist evocation of wild regions, (as in Auden's poetry of the English fells) mythic, Romantic. In this poem the Romantic element of experience, imagined wild places, humbles the pretensions of the mind for a poet who in *Leaving Barra* confessed himself

> *Restless as a gull and haunted*
> *By a hankering after Atlantis.*

Longing for such imaginative kingdoms is expressed with delicate poignancy in many of MacNeice's poems. Witness *Nostalgia* where natural events produce the dangerous longing

> *For what was never home ...*

The poem suggests that it is at times when the lamp is soft on the snow, that the will is vulnerable,

> *When homesick for the hollow*
> *Heart of the Milky Way*
> *The soundless clapper calls*
> *And we would follow ...*

Similar Romantic aspiration is present in the long poem *Autumn Sequel*, where desire for escape, for home, for the beyond, recurs in the midst of the tedium of urban professional duties:

> *We can still shake*
> *The circulars out of our hair and dive clean through*
> *These wells of ink to surface in a lake*
>
> *Two hundred miles away, two hundred fathoms blue.*

In that poem 'home'

> *is a place where things unheard*
> *Can be overheard; where, as tall stories tell,*
> *We find the Singing Tree and the Talking Bird,*
>
> *And what was lost when the ballet curtain fell.*

Romantic longing occurs even in the journalistic *Autumn Journal*, sometimes in an almost Poe-like determination (mingled with an ironic humour conveyed by the jingling rhythms) to escape the harsh facts of actuality, in a self-induced or alcoholic dream-world,

> *We'll get drunk among the roses*
> *In the valley of the moon ...*

while at other times his Romanticism is expressed in delicate images of another reality calling and beckoning to him like a voice from an alternative world, the world perceived by the imagination :

> *Who is it calls me*
> *When the cold draught picks my sleeve?*
> *Or sneezing in the morning sunlight or smelling the*
> *bonfire*
> *Over the webbed lawn and naked cabbage plot?*

Faced by the problems of the political world, and poverty and impending doom, he can permit himself the question,

> *While we sleep, what shall we dream?*
> *Of Tir nan Og or South Sea islands,*
> *Of a land where all the milk is cream*
> *And all the girls are willing?*

In MacNeice's very fine love poems the Romantic element in his sensibility received its freest rein. These often express a frank desire for an ideal love, for La Belle Dame Sans Merci, for that perfection and fulfilment in love which will transcend the actualities of time and place, baptising the present. Such longing is expressed beautifully in *Woods* where he permits himself to imagine the wood of romance 'a kingdom free from time and sky'. A similar desire is expressed most movingly in *Perdita* :

> *Somewhere or other a green*
> *Flag is waving under an iron vault*
> *And a brass bell is the herald of green country*
> *And the wind is in the wires and the broom is gold.*

Images suggestive of romance, legend, grounded in the everyday particulars of a railway station, conjoin with images of Romantic fulfilment in a passage of imaginative reverie, to reappear as an image of possible achievement in a later poem :

> *I shall leave the path and dismount*
> *From the mad-eyed beast and keep my appointment*
> *In green improbable fields with you.*

This free rein to Romantic feeling recurs in many of MacNeice's love poems. *Flowers in the Interval* is a moving example, where in its fourth section, the poet meditates on his lover's voice, breaking into an evocation of a Romantic past,

Through which forgotten
Ladies in wimple, ruff or hoop
Bonnet or bustle, take the air . . .

Romantic image follows Romantic image in a sustained passage
of unbridled imaginative reverie :

Of whom, thus launched, one rocks a firelit
Cradle beside a dying fire,
One wanders moonstruck on the fells . . .

The allusion to Coleridge's *To Dejection: An Ode* and to Wordsworth's *Lucy Gray* is clear, while the sound of his lover's voice
and the intensity of feeling it evokes, are mediated in images
of Romantic suggestiveness :

like a bird
Returned from a land I did not know
Making unheard-of meanings heard
And sprinkling all my days with daylight.

More usually, however, such unfettered, free flowering of a
Romantic sensibility is rare in MacNeice's verse. He is often
restricted to a Romantic longing and desire for that ideal true
realm of the imagination which the English Romantics thought
they were approaching, apprehending and making known in
their poetry.

MacNeice's Romanticism makes itself felt only in expressions
of longing and in brief snatches of imaginative license. It is as
if for a moment the sceptical eyes so firmly set on the real
world, film over, and the poet has a vision of some other
imaginative world of beauty and meaning. But such flowering
is held in check. It seems governed by the poet's awareness of
danger in Romantic escapism. His dreaming is always counter-
acted by an attitude represented in *Ode* :

I must put away this drug.

Must become the migrating bird following felt routes
The comet's superficially casual orbit kept
Not self-abandoning to sky-blind chutes
To climb miles and kiss the miles of foam . . .

For MacNeice knows that Romanticism is a 'drug'. This is more than superficial disillusion. Time and time again in MacNeice's verse, a Romantic dream world is created only to be cruelly crushed by the harshness of fact; the coloured delicate bubbles of the imagination are summarily burst by the deflating pins of actuality—scepticism undercuts all dreams. An obvious example of this is the poem in *Novelettes*, Les Sylphides. A man takes his girl to the ballet. The first irony is in line two :

> *Being shortsighted himself could hardly see it . . .*

The occasion provides for him a vision of ecstatic beauty. His beatification is, however, self-created, an effect of shortsightedness.

> *Calyx upon calyx, canterbury bells in the breeze*
> *The flowers on the left mirror to the flowers on the*
> *right . . .*

He also dreams of an ideal love, once more a myopic hope :

> *Now, he thought, we are floating—ageless, oarless—*
> *Now there is no separation, from now on*
> *You will be wearing white*
> *Satin and a red sash*
> *Under the waltzing trees.*

But the vision induced by bad sight fades, the dream gives away to cold fact :

> *So they were married—to be the more together—*
> *And found they were never again so much together . . .*

and all that is left is a poignant nostalgia for the fled vision :

> *And where were the white flowers.*

Irony is at work throughout the poem to suggest that only a myopic innocent would dream of ideal beauty, ideal love, time-lessness. But even a short-sighted dreamer has sight enough for the 'tradesman's bills'. No Romantic trance can banish their insistent encroachments.[3] Axel's Castle crumbles at one stroke of the bailiff's knock. *The Drunkard* is equally a poem of Romantic disillusion. It dramatises the moment of awakening from the visionary moment to the bitter facts of existence. The poem

echoes (indeed almost parodies) Keats's *Ode to a Nightingale*
where the doleful pealing of the word 'forlorn' had wrested that
poet back from the timeless song of the nightingale to the doubts
and questions of his waking self. The famous transition from the
penultimate to the last stanza of Keats's ode is echoed early
in MacNeice's poem. In stanza one the vision is fading fast.
The sense of unity he has experienced through inebriation
begins to

> *disperse*
> *On a sickly wind which drives all wraiths pell-mell*
> *Through tunnels to their appointed, separate places,*
>
> *And he is separate too ...*

The word 'separate' is repeated cleverly, heavily reinforcing
the harshness of fact, as opposed to the soft mystic beauty of
the visionary experience. With the repetition of 'separate' the
drunkard's 'hour-gone sacrament of drunkenness' is ended. The
vision is placed firmly in the past in the rest of the poem. He
had 'ascended into the hierarchy of created things'; reality had
taken on a new, an all-embracing unity; it had been religiously
apprehended; the customary had been transformed into something rich and strange :

> *The barmaid was a Madonna, the adoration*
> *Of the coalman's breath was myrrh, the world was We*
> *And pissing under the stars an act of creation*
> *While the low hills lay purring round the inn.*

The poem, however, has a satiric edge, foreign to the earnest
religiosity of Keats's flight of ecstatic mysticism, for from the
outset we are reminded that it is no valid vision, but a 'false
coin', the temporary, self-induced beatification which alcohol
provides.

   This kind of undercutting of a Romantic dream by a hard
uncompromising realism is a frequent attitude in MacNeice's
poetry at all stages in his poetic career. It suggests a poet attracted
by dreams, but sceptical of them. In his early poem *Eclogue
between the Motherless,* character A in the conversation longs
for the perfect, ideal love but discovers

> *all I wanted*
> *Was to get really close but closeness was*
> *Only a glove on the hand, alien and veinless . . .*

Dream and disillusion stand together in the poem, *The Hebrides,* ideal world and cold uncompromising fact in stark juxtaposition :

> *The fish come singing from the drunken sea,*
> *The herring rush the gunwales and sort themselves*
> *To cram the expectant barrels of their own accord—*
> *Or such is the dream of the fisherman whose wet*
> *Leggings hang on the door as he sleeps returned*
> *From a night when miles of net were drawn up empty.*

Ode, especially its opening, reveals how closely Romantic aspiration and an inveterate scepticism are related in MacNeice's sensibility. This poem is in fact a prayer for his son, and stands in obvious relationship to Yeats's poem *A Prayer for my Daughter.* It is instructive to compare the opening stanzas of the two poems. I place the Yeats stanza first :

> *Once more the storm is howling, and half hid*
> *Under this cradle-hood and coverlid*
> *My child sleeps on. There is no obstacle*
> *But Gregory's wood and one bare hill*
> *Whereby the haystack-and-roof-levelling wind,*
> *Bred on the Atlantic, can be stayed;*
> *And for an hour I have walked and prayed*
> *Because of the great gloom that is in my mind.*

> *To-night is so coarse with chocolate*
>   *The wind blowing from Bournville*
> *That I hanker after the Atlantic*
>   *With a frivolous nostalgia*
> *Like that which film-fans feel*
>   *For their celluloid abstractions*
> *The nifty hero and the deathless blonde*
>   *And find escape by proxy*
> *From the eight-hour day or the wheel*
>   *Of work and bearing children.*

The clear ancestor of the two poems is the conversation-poetry of Coleridge and more particularly his poem *Frost at Midnight;* but how much closer to Coleridge is the stanza by Yeats than that by MacNeice. There is the same creation of an essentially Romantic setting—a man meditating alone at night, aware only of the workings of Nature beyond him and the workings of his own consciousness in solitude. The openings of both Coleridge's and Yeats's poems are very moving, in their suggestion of a momentary stasis of man and nature, before the mind sets off on its solitary journey of meditation. MacNeice allows himself no such experience, no haunting confrontation of the solitary man before the forces of nature, as a setting for his meditation. Instead of the howling storm or the 'secret ministry of frost', the night 'is so coarse with chocolate' because the wind is blowing from Bournville—a chocolate factory. Yet MacNeice is more than the slick cynic parodying Yeats; there is the stuff of the Romantic in him, so he admits,

> *That I hanker after the Atlantic . . .*

that same Atlantic that bred the 'haystack-and-roof-levelling wind' of Yeats's poem. But as if to knock down any Romantic associations as soon as they rear their heads he adds

> *With a frivolous nostalgia . . .*

The bludgeon of disillusion is applied, and lest the force of nostalgia should seem other than frivolous, he elaborates the trite, rather laboured simile of the film fans' longing for their impossible idols, their 'celluloid abstractions'. Where Coleridge and Yeats created Romantic settings for their conversation-poem meditations in serious, solemn, quiet-toned poetry, MacNeice in rather mannered, slick verse creates an anti-Romantic setting for his largely similar meditation, and promptly knocks on the head any Romantic associations that are evoked, any flowering of the Romantic tendencies in his own sensibility with a cynical simile.

The poet is of course wise not to trust his imagination, for the history of Romantic exploit is a history of persistent shipwreck. The Romantic sensibility in the last one hundred and fifty years has proved on its pulses the powerful accuracy of Baudelaire's apprehension :

> *So, revelling, Imagination sails*
> *To find but a reef when dawn breaks on the sea.*[4]

In English poetry the poet who exemplified this shipwreck most clearly, was in fact Coleridge. His poetry was a record of failing faith in the power of the imagination to apprehend what Nature can give to the perceptive heart. Coleridge's experience can also be seen as a paradigm for the experience of the English Romantic imagination in general, during the nineteenth and the twentieth centuries, in face of the encroachments of the new sciences, the increase in urban civilisation, and the growth of technology. For the real world grew more and more beyond the imagination's power for re-creation, as poet after poet discovered, and Romantic faith in the power of the imagination was slowly lost. From the self-assurance of Wordsworth's declarations of faith, we move in the nineteenth century to the broken despairing notes of Matthew Arnold, the agnostic hesitancies and questionings of Tennyson, and to Browning's dramatic monologues, with their nervous, experimenting perspectivism. In our time the collapse of Romantic faith is almost complete and all that remains for the Romantic sensibility is frequent nostalgia for a time when its development was possible, at some period in the past (usually before the Industrial Revolution) or, more seldom, at some time in the poet's life, when all that is implied by the Romantic doctrine of the imagination was unknowingly experienced. It was Ruskin who first attributed the rise of Romantic passion for Nature to the Industrial Revolution, a perception that has since become a cultural commonplace, expressing itself in almost all the arts in primitivist movements, and culturally in a plentitude of enthusiastic cults which reject the dubious material gains of our own century for a rustic spirituality. The nostalgia of many modern poets is perhaps of a more special kind, though it is related to this more widespread variety. Conceiving of the function of poetry in terms derived very firmly from the Romantic-symbolist tradition, they sought, (Eliot, and Yeats in particular) as Professor Kermode has shown in his brilliant essay *Romantic Image*, an explanation for the sense of dislocation modern experience forced upon them. Believing, in Romantic fashion, that poetry must bring the whole soul of man into activity in a constant amalgamation of disparate experience, with, as Yeats desired, 'blood, imagination, intellect running together',[5] they sought historic explanation for the fact that this happy state of affairs clearly did not prevail in their own writing. They sought such explanation in a nostalgic survey of the past, to excuse their own failure to achieve the desired synthesis of intellect and emotion. It is the times that are at fault, not the poet. Frank Kermode expresses it succinctly: 'They seek, in short, a historical period possessing the qualities they postulate for the Image: unity, indissociability; qualities which, though passionately desired, are, they say, uniquely hard to come by in the modern world.'[6]

MacNeice displays a similar Romantic nostalgia in his poetry. He too looks to a time when, in his view, the ideals expressed by the Romantic poets were attainable. He laments the passing of a time when 'unity of being' was possible and more generally he is nostalgic about a past which seems preferable to the drab present. His own childhood is, interestingly, the main locus of idealised retrospection. Here he seems more akin to the major Romantic poets of the early nineteenth century than do many of the dissatisfied spirits of more recent times who have located their ideal society in the historic past (of these Arnold in the last century and Eliot in our own, are possibly the most obvious examples). Of course he also imagines, in typical Romantic fashion (the poem is *Autumn Journal*) a pre-industrial England when

> *Things were different when men felt their programme*
> *In the bones and pulse, not only in the brain . . .*

but more characteristically he writes of the blessedness of childhood, without the scepticism that underlines his evocation of the Romantic-historic past.

> *Oh, we know that the word merry*
> *Is vulgarised and Chaucer's England was not*
> *All cakes and ale nor all our childhood happy;*
> *Still there is something lost. The very limitedness*
> *Of childhood, its ignorance, its impotence,*
> *Made every cockcrow a miracle after the ogre's night*
> *And every sunbeam glad—as the medieval winter*
> *Slow and dense with cold made March a golden avatar,*
> *April Adam's innocence and May maiden's gaiety . . .*
>
> > *(The Stygian Banks)*

It is to the 'ignorance' of childhood that the Romantic nostalgic in MacNeice's nature turned time and again in poetry, remembering it as a time of 'felt unity'.

MacNeice's poetry of childhood is both escapist and exploratory; it partly expressed escapist nostalgia for past experiences, and partly explored the peculiar unity, which is the poet's idealised version of childhood experience. In a section of exploratory verse in *The Stygian Banks* he theorises on childhood:

> *Munching salad*
> *Your child can taste the colour itself—the green—*
> *And the colour of radish—the red; his jaded parents,*
> *Wise to the fallacy, foster it (for we begin with*
> *A felt unity . . .*

This 'felt unity', when the whole soul of man was in activity, 'blood, imagination, intellect, running together' when the intellect and experience were undissociated, is remembered nostalgically in many of MacNeice's poems of childhood. The simplest, but to my mind most effective treatment of this theme is the poem *Autobiography*. Its simplicity of expression captures the intensity of physical sensation in childhood, in the same way as the first few pages of Joyce's *A Portrait of the Artist as a Young Man*. The thrilling shock of sensation is evoked in the lines

> *In my childhood trees were green*
> *And there was plenty to be seen.*
> . . . .
> *My father made the walls resound,*
> *He wore his collar the wrong way round.*

The moment of fracture, the breaking of the magic spell, is suggested by a diction of compelling simplicity, reminiscent of that used by Wordsworth to such effect in his poem on the waning of imaginative powers, *Ode on the Intimations of Immortality*.

> *I got up; the chilly sun*
> *Saw me walk away alone.*

The haunting refrain has a special troubling power:

> *Come back early or never come.*

This simplicity is not facile. It suggests an experience lost, an experience so precious that words scarcely can cope with its disappearance. In *Twelfth Night*, perhaps not with quite the same superb simplicity, but to moving effect, MacNeice evokes the lost realm of childhood, and suggests its fragile transience by an extended trope of the swift melting of winter snow. He captures once more the vividness of sense impression, in onomatopoeic lines :

> *O crunch of bull's-eyes in the mouth,*
> *O crunch of frost beneath the foot—*

and affirms the 'felt unity' that is experienced in childhood :

> *O harmony of roof and hedge,*
> *O parity of sight and thought—*
> *And each flake had your number on it.*

But throughout the poem is the bitter knowledge that the snow must melt, until the last stanza speaks with wistful, delicate nostalgia for fled vision.

> *For now the time of gifts is gone—*
> *O boys that grow, O snows that melt,*
> *O bathos that the years must fill.*

This is very poignant. The poem concludes with the hard admission

> *Here is dull earth to build upon*
> *Undecorated . . .*

The dream is shattered, the Romantic hope of re-creating the world in each instant by the power of imagination, quite dissipated. Another poem that presents the unified world of childhood experience is *When we were Children*. It posits that in childhood experience, language and its referents seemed intertwined, inextricably linked in some rich and fecund unity.

> *When we were children words were coloured*
> *(Harlot and murder were dark purple) . . .*

In such experience intellectual apprehension and sensory perception are identical. In the second stanza perception is presented

D

in lines where the senses are confused, suggesting that sight is so intense that it is scarcely distinguishable from taste,

> *When we were children Spring was easy,*
> *Dousing our heads in suds of hawthorn*
> *And scrambling the laburnum tree—*
> *A breakfast for the gluttonous eye . . .*

The final stanza presents the grim experience of the disillusion that comes with age and the passage of time. Cerebration and intellectual abstraction destroy the beautiful unified world of childhood :

> *Now we are older and our talents*
> *Accredited to time and meaning . . .*

It will require something new to re-create the lost world where word and object were so synthesised, so that

> *meaning shall remarry colour*
> *And flowers be timeless once again.*

It seems odd that MacNeice's sister should write (in a note to the autobiographical fragment *The Strings are False*), in comment on the poem *Autobiography*, 'I think that the shock of seeing the sudden change in the mother whom he loved so much, followed by the uncertainty of her return, may have been the chief factor which caused Louis's memories of childhood to be so sad and sometimes so bitter.'[7] For although he does present 'the black dreams' that tormented him in childhood, more usually his poetical reminiscences of childhood are those of a man looking nostalgically to a time of blessedness, a time of 'unity of being'. There is something almost Wordsworthian in his obsessive nostalgia for childhood, which sets him apart from his contemporaries with the exception of Dylan Thomas who also wrote most movingly of his nostalgic memories of a blissful childhood.

MacNeice however is under no illusions. He does not use his memories of childhood experience to fortify himself against the cold drabness of fact. For MacNeice is a modern man, a sceptical poet, a cold-eyed realist. It is interesting to note that when he was at school in England he could write like a latter-day Romantic. In his book *Modern Poetry* he quotes from an essay he wrote when he was a schoolboy: 'The dwellers in Xanadu never saw a van going down the street and piled with petrol tins in beautiful reds and yellows and green . . . This age is as *romantically interesting* [italics added later] as any other age . . .'[8] When he wrote his adult poetry he no longer found much of the present age 'romantically interesting'. Equipped with much that goes to form a Romantic sensibility, usually he did not write as a Romantic, except in sporadic flashes, in brief holidays from ironic watchfulness and sceptical disillusion.

2

The Modern Sensibility

MR ANTHONY THWAITE once wrote of MacNeice, that he had a Romantic sensibility 'modified and qualified by all that has come into existence since the early nineteenth century'.[1] MacNeice's Romantic sensibility was, I would suggest, almost extinguished by the modern world in which he wrote. For the situation by which the modern poet is confronted is one where faith of any kind is difficult if not impossible.

To attempt to outline what characterises contemporary civilisation is a foolhardy enterprise. W. H. Auden, attempting to describe our world to Lord Byron in *Letters from Iceland,* remarked:

> *far too much has happened since your death.*
> *Crying went out and the cold bath came in,*
> *With drains, bananas, bicycles and tin,*
> *And Europe saw from Ireland to Albania*
> *The Gothic revival and the Railway Mania.*

Certain things are, however, fairly clear. Urban development has mushroomed appallingly. Our physical environment is changing daily:

> *A world of Aertex underwear for boys,*
> *Huge plate-glass windows, walls absorbing noise . . .*

Yet the outward, environmental changes are perhaps merely indicative of, and attendant upon changes in ideas and basic assumptions. The last hundred and fifty years have seen the growth of sciences of all kinds: biological, physical, chemical, anthropological and psychological. The effects of this are wittily satirised by Auden:

Nothing, says science, is impossible:
The Pope may quit to join the Oxford Groupers . . .

More seriously, this growth in certain forms of knowledge has helped to create an atmosphere of enervating relativism. The new sciences dominating men's awareness create a relativistic, deterministic world-picture. J. Hillis Miller, in his book on Victorian poetry, identifies this 'modern spirit' as follows: 'To be a victim of the "modern spirit" means to be forced to conduct oneself according to inherited institutions, beliefs, laws, and customs, which no longer seem appropriate to actual conditions, and it means doubt of the possibility of ever finding the proper form of life.'[2] In such a situation any commitment, belief, or act of faith (whether in God, in politics, or the power of the imagination) is made difficult. It is this loss of values to live by, which is implied in Nietzsche's famous declaration that the Deity is no more. This awareness is not greeted by all with the joy that it sometimes, apparently, afforded Nietzsche. As a cultural phenomenon the 'death of God' is being lived by Western European civilisation in our century. A modern theologian puts it succinctly: 'If there is one clear portal to the twentieth century, it is a passage through the death of God, the collapse of any meaning or reality lying beyond the newly discovered radical immanence of modern man, an immanence dissolving even the memory or shadow of transcendence.'[3]

MacNeice wrote a number of poems that specifically discuss this loss of religious faith in our time. Their tone is something far beyond a fashionable, agnostic hesitancy, for they display a serious awareness of the dereliction such loss must occasion. Perhaps in our world religious scepticism is the only possible option, and to a poet reared firmly in the Christian tradition, and haunted by its images (many of his poems employ Christian images and symbols), this could not be an easy admission. In *Autumn Journal* he questions:

Whom shall we pray to?
Shall we give like decadent Athens the benefit of the
doubt
To the Unknown God or smugly pantheistic
Assume that God is everywhere round about?
But if we assume such a God, then who the devil
Are these with empty stomachs or empty smiles?

We must not let the colloquial expression or the thirtyish mode of such a passage blind us to the concern with which MacNeice asks such questions. The difficulty of faith in God so stated, nineteen lines later the poet admits:

> *It is December now, the trees are naked*
> *As the three crosses on the hill . . .*

In the Christmas month a vision of a naked cross, we celebrate not the birth of God but his death. In *Whit Monday*

> *The Bank (if you call it a holiday) Holiday crowds*
> *Stroll from street to street, cocking an eye*
> *For where the angel used to be in the sky . . .*

The Return considers the departed faith: the attitude is tensely ambivalent:

> *All the birds that flew and left the big sky empty,*
> *Come back throwing shadows on our patience.*

Stanza two is heavy with false termination, with dissatisfaction in the present:

> *Bethlehem is desolate and the stables*
> *Cobwebbed, mute; below each Tower of Babel's*
> *Sentrydom of night, inside the bleak*
> *Glass of cafés chairs are piled on tables.*

In *Autumn Sequel* the poet thinks of 'the great No-God' and claims

> *This is the age*
> *He has made his own by making nothing in it*
> *Appear worth while . . .*

while in *Jigsaws* he realises that perhaps we need a transcendent God to give value to the events of our lives:

> *Let the skew runner breast the tape,*
> *Let the great lion leave his lair,*
> *Let the hot nymph solicit rape,*
> *We need a God to phrase it fair;*
> *. . . .*
> *We need one Name to take in vain,*
> *One taboo to break, one sin to dare.*

Place of a Skull most directly confronts the death of God. It identifies the world of physical existence with the seamless coat of Christian legend. When Christ dies ('the weaver who had made night and day') the soldiers dice for the seamless coat, only to discover, its owner dead, the coat is frayed, worthless.

> *The dice were gay*
> *And someone won:* Why the first time I wore
> That dead man's coat it frayed I cannot say.

MacNeice's view of the modern world as we see it in the poetry, a sceptical concerned pain which no single religious faith can alleviate, for a time placed him among the group of poets in the thirties which became known as the 'Pylon School'. It is of course a misnomer to call this group a 'school' for it is even doubtful if they ever all met together in the same room, and although they felt a sort of kinship, one for the other (witness C. Day Lewis's discussion of his fellow poets in his book *A Hope for Poetry*) it is now certain that they themselves were unaware of forming anything so clear-cut as a 'school'.

Stephen Spender in his pamphlet *Poetry Since 1939*, wrote of the group : 'They were not in a deliberate sense a literary movement; they were rather a group of friends, contemporaries at the Universities of Oxford and Cambridge, influenced by each other in a personal way.'[4] Some remarks by W. H. Auden reinforce the point : 'From a literary point of view, the customary journalistic linkage of the names Auden, Day Lewis, MacNeice, Spender, is, and always was absurd. Even when we seemed to share some common concern—political let us say, our approaches to it, our sensibilities and techniques were always different.'[5] The attitudes of this group may be fairly represented by Spender's poem *Who Live under the Shadow* :

> *Who live under the shadow of a war,*
> *What can I do that matters?*[6]

and by his poem *Oh Young Men.*

> *Oh young men oh young comrades*
> *it is too late now to stay in those houses*
> *your fathers built where they built you to build to breed*
> *money on money.*[7]

They were each highly critical of existing capitalist society, conscious of impending doom, of a way of life coming to an end, and some of them were firmly committed to a socialist revolution. They were not alone in their apocalyptic feelings. Many besides the 'Pylon poets' felt that the end of a civilsation was at hand. Graham Greene could write in 1934 'Whatever the political changes in this country during the next few years one thing is surely almost certain : the class distinctions will not remain un-altered and the public school, as it exists to-day, will disappear.'[8] This may seem somewhat disappointing as apocalypse but as Symons points out in *The Thirties*, the demise of the public school system represented for many intellectuals in the thirties the beginnings of deeply significant changes in the total structure of society. Most of them had in fact been educated in public schools and these represented for them the bastions of established order. MacNeice gives us his somewhat disdainful, brilliantly witty account of his own public school education in *Autumn Journal*.

Much of MacNeice's early poetry is informed with fashion-able apocalyptic tones. In *An Eclogue for Christmas* we meet the familiar prophecies of the end of bourgeois civilisation :

> *The jaded calendar revolves,*
> *Its nuts need oil, carbon chokes the valves,*
> *The excess sugar of a diabetic culture*
> *Rotting the nerve of life and literature . . .*

Long, ranging rhythms convey a sense of tired, debilitated culture :

> *It is time for some new coinage, people have got so*
> *old,*
> *Hacked and handled and shiny from pocketing they have*
> *made bold*
> *To think that each is himself through these accidents . . .*

The poet asserts that 'things draw to an end, the soil is stale' while he senses in *Autumn Journal* that ' "This is the end of the old regime" '. A decaying civilisation awaits the revolutionary cleansing :

What will happen when the sniggering machine-guns in
the hands of the young men
Are trained on every flat and club and beauty parlour and
Father's den?

This is in the conventional thirties mode; any of the left-wing verse of the period would supply analogues. Yet MacNeice is unique in this group in conveying a sense of total doom. Most of the others had creeds to explain the approaching catastrophe. Usually in MacNeice's early verse there is only the sense of doom, the certainty that the sea will engulf them :

Come then all of you, come closer, form a circle,
Join hands and make believe that joined
Hands will keep away the wolves of water
Who howl along our coast. And be it assumed
That no one hears them among the talk and laughter.

(Wolves)

The sense of doom finds its most compelling expression in two very different poems. In a moving lyric *The Sunlight on the Garden* MacNeice offers a tender statement of what will be lost in the inevitable situation that advances :

When all is told
We cannot beg for pardon.

Our freedom as free lances
Advances towards its end . . . .

The other poem is a rollicking bitter satire in which all anodynes are recognised as ineffectual in the knowledge of a doom-laden future. The bagpipes of *Bagpipe Music* screech a message of total despair; its notes are irrefutable.

The glass is falling hour by hour, the glass will fall for
ever,
But if you break the bloody glass you won't hold up the
weather.

The classification of MacNeice as a poet of the 'Pylon School', a left-wing poet who looked in the thirties to the coming revolution is simplistic. For in political as well as in metaphysical and religious matters, his scepticism was fundamental. Throughout his early poetry there is the expression of a scepticism that any creed or system would prove adequate in the existing social situation or in the coming catastrophe. This scepticism is frequently the mood of *Autumn Journal,* the remarkable poem MacNeice wrote in 1938, and it finds its most explicit statement in the poem *To a Communist* :

> *But before you proclaim the millennium, my dear,*
> *Consult the barometer—*
> *This poise is perfect but maintained*
> *For one day only.*

MacNeice wrote of his political scepticism of the thirties in *The Strings are False.* At one point he describes the left-wing mecca provided by his landlady's home in Birmingham :

> Many Leftist writers came to stay in her house—Maurice Dobb, A. L. Rowse, John Strachey, Naomi Mitchison. The word Proletariat hung in festoons from the ceiling. And yet I felt that they were all living in the study. The armchair reformist sits between two dangers—wishful thinking and self-indulgent gloom. The phrase 'I told you so' is near to his heart (the *New Statesman and Nation,* our leading Leftist weekly, lived upon prophecies of disaster—and was never disappointed) but when he fancies an allegro movement he has—or had, rather—only to turn to Moscow. Naomi Mitchison after a fortnight or so in Russia gave a lecture at Birmingham University about the joy in the faces of the masses. It all seemed to me too pat. Our Landlady's friends had a gospel-tent enthusiasm and quivers of prickly statistics, but the gospel of Marx as sifted through Transport House seemed to me hardly more inspiring or broad-minded than the gospels of Dr. Arnold or Cecil Rhodes.[9]

This echoes the political scepticism of the poetry. To these remarks could be added MacNeice's statements in *The Poetry of W. B. Yeats* : 'Yeats, like Eliot, assumes that a world built upon communist principles would imply a mechanical equality, a drab uniformity. It is hoped that this is a wrong assumption, though it is supported by many examples so far given of communist *intellectual* dictatorship, of the wholesale issue of machine-made and trade-marked opinions . . . The left wing intellectual, before he throws a stone at them, should consider whether his own motives for advocating 'the classless society' are disinterested.'[10] Many years later MacNeice wrote of the hypocrisy of much of the left-wing commitment of the late twenties and thirties: 'Take, for instance, the question of class. There were many undergraduates like myself who theoretically conceded that all men are equal, but who, in practice, while only too willing to converse, or attempt to, with say Normandy peasants or shop-keepers, would wince away in their own college halls from those old grammar school boys who with impure vowels kept admiring Bernard Shaw or Noel Coward while grabbing their knives and forks like dumb-bells'.[11] Such humorously expressed scepticism and analytic honesty is usually unwelcome in the ranks of the politically committed. And MacNeice is only slightly related to the left-wing movement of the thirties. He shared the left wing's distaste for the existing system but lacked its faith in a solution. The mood of the poetry is certainly often similar to that in more overtly socialist verse, but it is in fact his plays that, to my mind, most clearly stamp MacNeice as a thirties writer. This is surely because drama is the more public medium, in which the poet was more likely to reflect contemporary public concerns. *Out of the Picture* (for example) contains a number of poems which for a reader in the seventies, who was not alive in the thirties, evoke most clearly what he imagines that period to have been like. *Pindar is Dead* is particularly effective. The impression which the play creates is of a somewhat frenzied attempt to get everything in—airports and Freud, cigarette-lighters, fried eggs and Marx. The play itself is very dated and must be judged a failure in F. O. Matthiessen's terms: 'the one occasion where MacNeice seems to have collapsed into being affected by the least valuable elements in Auden, and has produced a loosely blurred mixture where it is hard to say whether the intention is satire or farce, since nothing comes through clear.'[12]

Station Bell, an unpublished play, written and performed in Birmingham, is similarly confused. One has the feeling reading the typescript that the writer uses the play to include every contemporary cultural gimmick, as an undergraduate essay will display its writer's knowledge, whether relevant or not. The play is set in a station bar. A female named Julia Brown declares herself dictator of Ireland, having survived a communist bomb attack. Her revenue is gained by the export of a drink brewed from seaweed. The newly established dictator arranges a plot against one O'Halloran who is to be made a national scapegoat at their next rally, Jews being a distinct rarity. A propaganda corps is formed, made up of a Drummer, Conjuror, Cardsharper, Bearded Lady, Jew and Epileptic. The play proceeds with this hotchpotch of burlesque and comedy tied together by a minimum of plot, until the unlikely climax in which Julia Brown unmasks a plot to blow up the train in which she and a clergyman were escaping to America.

The fashionable association of MacNeice with the other, more convinced left-wing poets, is easily explained. It is simply that MacNeice's distaste for the modern world, for the 'frayed robe' of modern civilisation, (coupled with a leaning towards the Left in sympathy),[13] produced temporary similarities in outlook and attitudes to dogmatic leftist poets, who were also bitterly critical of society.

MacNeice abhors many aspects of modernity. He detests mass production. In *Belfast* he distastefully lists the synthetic products; *Jigsaws* includes a vigorous attack on the artificial sterility of our civilisation while *Memoranda to Horace* satirises contemporary medical-sexual mores. The most complete statement of the poet's utter distaste for the artificial is the poem *In Lieu*, where a civilisation founded on cheap artifice is denounced.

> *Roses with the scent bred out,*
> *In lieu of which is a long name on a label.*
> *Dragonflies reverting to grubs,*
> *Tundra and desert overcrowded,*
> *And in lieu of a high altar*
> *Wafers and wine procured by a coin in a slot.*

In his radio plays MacNeice frequently attacked Science and her works, that Science which had rendered mass production possible. In *The Mad Islands* the Inventor, who stirs a cauldron from which comes 'the tickings and hummings of modern technology',[14] is vigorously satirised, while in the stage play *One for the Grave* Science is symbolised by the metallic voice of an electronic brain which prophesies instant Utopia :

> *But Science today is the high road to Paradise,*
> *high road to Paradise, high road to Paradise,*
> *Science today is the high road to Paradise,*
> *Now and till Kingdom come.*[15]

In this debased culture individuality is annihilated. In the final section of *Autumn Journal* the poet's millenial aspirations therefore include the hope of a society,

> *Where life is a choice of instruments and none*
> *Is debarred his natural music . . .*

So in *Refugees* exiles flee to be themselves. The fear of the unborn child in *Prayer before Birth* is partly of the destruction of his individuality. *The Kingdom* praises individuals, sets them against a world where individuality is threatened. In *Autumn Sequel* the poet states of the mass of men:

> *Theirs is the age and theirs*
> *The vast assurance of the automaton . . .*

and satirises the conformity of contemporary suburbia, while praising those individuals 'who still defy' this 'brash new age and thus redeem our days from uniform sterility'. In *Memoranda to Horace* he praises the individuals with whom he can be human:

> *Which yet means relief from the false identity*
> *Assumed in the day and the city, the pompous*
> *Cold stereotype that you in your period*
> *Tried to escape in your Sabine farmhouse.*

The city too appals MacNeice. A partly topographical poem like *Birmingham* conveys the poet's distaste for the urban world. The poem captures the glowering, powerful menace of an industrial landscape (as well as its occasional beauty). But it is not only the appearance of the city that appals MacNeice. He is even more disturbed by its influence on the quality of our lives. *The Hebrides*, celebrating life on those lonely islands, by implication and by statement criticises the life of the city. On those islands 'no one hurries'; its inhabitants share 'Instinctive wisdom' and, primarily, on those islands the art of being a stranger with your neighbour

> *Has still to be imported . . .*
>
> *. . . .*
>
> *. . . no train runs on rails and the tyrant time*
> *Has no clock-towers to signal people to doom . . .*

Refugees presents the impersonality of the city :

> *And meanwhile the city will go on, regardless*
> *Of any new arrival, trains like prayers*
> *Radiating from stations haughty as cathedrals,*
> *Tableaux of spring in milliners' windows . . .*

Aftermath mourns London's loss of community feeling after the Second World War, while *Jigsaws* satirises suburban mediocrity :

> *A box to live in, with airs and graces,*
> *A box on wheels that shows its paces,*
> *A box that talks or that makes faces,*
> *And curtains and fences as good as the neighbours'*
> *To keep out the neighbours and keep us immured . . .*

MacNeice takes leave of the city in a moving poem *Good-bye to London*. The poem has a haunting lyrical refrain, redolent with poignant feeling. It indicts a total way of life.

> *And nobody rose, only some meaningless*
> *Buildings and the people once more were strangers*
> *At home with no one, sibling or friend.*
> *Which is why now the petals fall*
> *Fast from the flower of cities all.*

Throughout MacNeice's poetry, criticism of modernity is a constant. He detests the hectoring voices of the politicians. Perhaps they are leading us towards horror : 'O'Casey assumes that life is becoming more varied and colourful, but is it? The Welfare State is all very well but, if we look a little further ahead, we can foresee a subtopia which means *Standing Room Only* for everyone.'[16] He fears the castration of our culture by the mass media, since, as he suggests in a note to his modern morality play *One for the Grave* : 'it is the fate of the 20th Century Everyman to live in a world of mass media'. In *To Posterity* he fears a time

> *When books have all seized up like the books in graveyards*
> *And reading and even speaking have been replaced*
> *By other, less difficult, media . . .*

He unconditionally attacks stupidity and cant and is incredulous at the crass, damnable actions of men. He writes of the bombing of Hiroshima (in *Notes for a Biography*)

> *When I first read the news, to my shame I was glad;*
> *When I next read the news I thought man had gone*
> *mad . . .*

and he can only exclaim in despair at the utter diabolic folly of his contemporaries. MacNeice looks at them with a pained, despairing incredulity. But this 'frayed' world is where we must live and some cannot cope. MacNeice wrote sympathetically of those who stumble in the murk and mangle of modernity. Sometimes the lost are the sensitive and aware, like *The Conscript,* whose sensitivity to life's possibilities sets him apart from his peers. At other times the lost are those who have mistaken their identity, their true self, if it ever existed. Such a one is *The Mixer* whose sociability is a cloak for the hollowness he knows is at the centre of his personality. Others like *The Libertine* seek a satisfaction in the sexual life which cannot be attained. At a deeper level *The Suicide* is one who has suddenly become aware of the void of nihilism :

> *he stumbled*
> *Suddenly finally conscious of all he lacked*
> *On a manhole under the hollyhocks . . .*

But perhaps the most representative victim of the age is that dramatically presented in *The Springboard*, a modern Saint Thomas, racked by doubt and scepticism (MacNeice wrote two poems with Saint Thomas as their subject). He is unable to commit himself :

> *but it was more than fright*
> *That kept him crucified among the budding stars.*

> *Yes, it was unbelief.*

The modern predicament is imaged in this poem. In an age of historicism, relativism and resultant scepticism, the leap of faith is impossible, the life of commitment an unreasonable intellectual suicide.

> *He never made the dive—not while I watched.*

It may be noticed that many of these victims share a common predicament, solitude. Language provides little salve for the pain of their loneliness. It often provides communication without communion. This is a familiar theme in modern literature. It is obsessively treated by Sartre, Beckett, Pinter and many others. Iris Murdoch has written well of this modern sense of the failure of language: 'We can no longer take language for granted as a medium of communication. Its transparency has gone. We are like people who for a long time looked out of a window without noticing the glass—and then one day began to notice this too.'[17] MacNeice notices the glass. *Idle Talk* presents the problem (though it also moves towards a solution) of the 'little words that get in the way'. In *Babel* the poet asks

> *Can't we ever, my love, speak in the same language,*

and declares that we are 'Exiles all . . . in a foreign city'. The last stanza dramatises a world of unreal communication:

> *Patriots, dreamers, die-hards, theoreticians, all,*
> *Can't we ever, my love, speak in the same language,*
> *Or shall we go, still quarrelling over words, to the wall?*
> *Have we no aims in common?*

This is a subtle poem and bears examination. It depends for its effect on the use of cliché, or near cliché. The poet is addressing another person (his mistress) and he does so using lines that throughout suggest cliché and stock phrase. The first line 'There was a tower that went before a fall' suggests the familiar adage about pride. The phrase 'aims in common' is a familiar cliché, while 'The more there are together, Togetherness recedes' is a wittily ironic alteration of a song. 'Cut each other's throats' is a faded image, almost a cliché, while the image of going to the wall, in the penultimate line, is a flat banality, also a near cliché. This poem, presenting the difficulty of communication, is a subtle construct of cliché and faded imagery. Samuel Beckett, who is fascinated by the problems of the inadequacies of language, uses a similar technique in *Waiting for Godot* where much of the dialogue depends on a use of cliché and stock phrase. In his late poetry MacNeice employs speech of this kind where no true communication takes place. *The Taxis*, for example, suggests the disturbing illogicality of nightmare :

> *As for the fourth taxi, he was alone*
> *Tra-la when he hailed it but the cabby looked*
> *Through him and said: 'I can't tra-la well take*
> *So many people, not to speak of the dog.'*

Such a failure of faith in language, experienced by many twentieth-century artists and philosophers, may be understood as an expression of contemporary alienation, the philosophical sense of the contingency of the world and of the insurmountable duality in man's relation to his environment. Each man is locked up in the lonely isolation of his subjectivity; or so much modern thought and opinion would have us believe. The sources of this awareness are of course many (urbanisation plays an obvious part) but primary among them is the prevailing philosophic attitude of the past three hundred years. The age of self-consciousness dawned in the seventeenth century with the institutionalising of the rights of the private individual, whether political, scientific, religious or aesthetic. From this period we have the first of the self-conscious heroes, the meditative prince of Denmark—whatever the critic makes of *Hamlet* it seems clear that the prince thinks about himself rather a lot. Philosophically, the creator of modern self-consciousness is Descartes with his affirmation of the dualism between perceiving subject and perceived object. He conceived of the self as a logical rational entity which looked out at the world of objects, and which would, by the laws of logic and of science, explain what it saw. The self became separate from the world and has remained so in the majority of philosophic writings since. W. H. Auden has described the effect of this development :

Cartesian metaphysics, Newtonian physics and eighteenth-century theories of perception divided the body from the mind, and the primary objects of perception from their secondary qualities, so that physical nature became, as Professor Colling-

E

wood says 'matter, infinite in extent, permeated by movement, devoid of ultimate qualitative differences, and moved by uniform and purely quantitative forces', the colourless desert from which Melville recoils: 'All deified nature absolutely paints like a harlot, whose allurements cover nothing but the charnel house within; and when we proceed further, the palsied universe lies before us like a leper.'[18]

This revolution in philosophic thinking was vital for Western civilisation; it paved the way for the scientific revolution and material progress; but it has also helped to lead to the obsessional sense of isolation which is experienced by many in the twentieth century and which is treated in much of our literature.

The English Romantic poets responded vigorously to the early development of this sense of contingency, and their endeavours were in part an attempt to resolve the dualism. They, almost as disturbingly as any modern, were aware of themselves, and sensed that outside them was the cold, dead matter of the Newtonian universe. As John Bayley states, writing of them: 'It would be a reasonably safe generalisation to say that the premises on which any romantic poem is written are an acute consciousness of the isolated creating self on the one hand, and of a world unrelated, and possibly uninterested and hostile, on the other; and the wish somehow to achieve a harmonious synthesis of the two.'[19]

One obvious way to resolve the duality is to deny its existence. Much of the philosophy written since Descartes, a large proportion of which has been Idealist to varying degrees, has done this. If we can say that the only important reality is mind or subjectivity, we can forget the intractable external world or treat it as relatively unimportant, secondary. English Romanticism, particularly as manifested in the poetry of Wordsworth, had distinctly Idealist tendencies. The Romantic poet sometimes solved the dualism by ignoring one element of it. In the realm of the imagination, all dualisms are resolved. This stratagem of course had its problems, as John Bayley argued when he identified the source of Romantic insecurity:

Is the real world the domain of the poet's imagination, in which, like a king, it has its duties and responsibilities, or is the poet concerned only with a world perceived and created by

his own mind? In so far as the world is dead, stupid, intractable, a gross materialistic presence, may the poet ignore
it—or must he attempt to make all come to life under the
power of the imagination?[20]

Such is the problem and the Romantics attempted to resolve it
in their varying ways. Yet the era of obsessive intense self-
consciousness is still with us. We may even be more conscious
of a radical split between inner and outer world than the
Romantics were. In J. Hillis Miller's words: 'modern thought
has been increasingly dominated by the presupposition that each
man is locked in the prison of his consciousness'.[21] For it needed
only the loss of belief in God, in a transcendent reality, or
absolute, to transform Romantic subjective idealism, with its faith
in the high validity of imaginative experience, into a horrifying
solipsism. We sense the total isolation of the human self, its
separation from the world of matter. We are sceptical of the
imagination's power to impregnate or mould reality, and subjective idealism collapses into solipsism. The visions of the
imagination seem suspiciously similar to those of a neurotic
consciousness, not an insight into a transcendent, unified reality.

MacNeice's poetry clearly treats this central preoccupation
of modernity—the alienated self. He was obviously aware of the
problem as a comment on an incident in *Alice Through the
Looking Glass* reveals: 'This passage is not just the *jeu d'esprit*
of an Oxford don who has studied the traditional conundrums
of philosophy: it is also the rather moving dramatisation of one's
everyday discovery that selfhood cuts one off from the rest of
the universe.'[22] He further writes of another incident in the same
book: 'Thanks to Lewis Carroll's ease of manner the reader may
not notice that this is all near the bone: after all even the most
hard-headed business man has a solipsist inside him somewhere.'[23]
MacNeice, no hard-headed business man, admitted of his thinking when he was an undergraduate, 'Metaphysically, I was very
near solipsism.'[24] Clearly he felt the implacable, yet poignant,
logic of such a position. The poem that best exemplifies his preoccupation with this theme is *House on a Cliff*. It describes a
man in a house on a windy night. The dualism between subject
and object is evoked by the two polarities, indoors and out-
doors.

> *Indoors the sound of the wind. Outdoors the wind . . .*

while the isolation of a subjectivity which must be content with the sound of the wind is suggested in the line

> *Indoors the locked heart and the lost key.*

The disturbing possibility that perception may deceive is implicit in the last two lines :

> *Indoors a purposeful man who talks at cross*
> *Purposes, to himself, in a broken sleep.*

He hears only the noise of the wind while the wind itself may be entirely unknown. Human consciousness is a man asleep in a house on a cliff, dreaming to himself while the wind rages outside.

MacNeice presents this lonely isolation of the self in many poems. *The Lake in the Park* describes a clerk sculling alone on a lake, totally cut off from the vigorous natural life that surrounds him. The poem as an image is potent. It powerfully evokes the solitude of the self, the isolated subjectivity of a consciousness :

> *On the bank a father and mother goose*
> *Hiss as he passes, pigeons are courting,*
> *Everything mocks; the empty deck-chairs*
> *Are set in pairs, there is no consorting*
>
> *For him with nature or man . . .*

Note that all round him on the banks of the lake, from which he is cut off by a stretch of water, are signs of relationships, goose with goose, pigeon with pigeon, even chair with chair (suggesting a human courtship). He alone is isolated.

This awareness is most frequently suggested in MacNeice's poetry by imagery of windows. In many poems we find a man, or the poet, peering out at events and objects through a window, conscious of the intervening glass—of separation, division, of the dualism between the perceiver and the thing perceived :

Suspended in a moving night
The face in the reflected train
Looks at first sight as self-assured
As your own face—But look again:
Windows between you and the world
Keep out the cold; keep out the fright;
Then why does your reflection seem
So lonely in the moving night?

(Corner Seat)

The lonely self is cut off from the world. In *Train to Dublin* the poet remarks

outside my window here,
The smoke makes broken queries in the air.

The Window initially suggests that life can be seen as

Beginning your life with an overdraft, born looking out
on a surge of eroding
Objects . . .

The third poem of *Country Week-end* presents the poet

Watching through glass the trees blown east . . .

and remembering when as

a child I pressed
My nose against the streaming pane . . .

In *Windowscape* 'the panes are dusty' and the poem presents his own troubled subjectivity rather than what he sees outside. In *Solitary Travel* he explicitly admits his sense of being 'always under water or glass' tired by perpetual cerebration, alienated from the external world. *Restaurant Car* once more sees the poet on a train journey wondering

what
Mad country moves beyond the steamed-up window . . .

His curious mind ponders the essentially metaphysical problem as to what might be there, beyond the ever present glass.

The Wiper, another journey poem, is a sustained trope imaging the isolation of the alienated self. The car drives through the darkness:

> *Through purblind night the wiper*
> *Reaps a swathe of water*
> *On the screen; we shudder on*
>   *And hardly hold the road,*
> *All we can see a segment*
> *Of blackly shining asphalt*
> *With the wiper moving across it*
>   *Clearing, blurring, clearing.*

Charon presents the journey as it approaches the destination :

> *We moved through London,*
> *We could see the pigeons through the glass but failed*
> *To hear their rumours of wars . . .*

Throughout the poetry images of isolation recur. In *No More Sea* the self is a lonely island in an immense sea (which at least allows us freedom) :

> *Dove-melting mountains, ridges gashed with water,*
> *Itinerant clouds whose rubrics never alter*
> *Give, without oath, their testimony of silence*
> *To islanders whose hearts themselves are islands.*

Elsewhere the isolation is that of a bird in a cage as in *Budgie* where a bird sits on its burning perch and twitters 'I am' like a miniature Decartes,

> *there is only itself and the universe . . .*

Beyond is 'The small blue universe', perhaps a projection, (the budgie is a 'small blue bundle') a subjective idealist construct of the mind, or, perhaps 'something different' :

> *Galaxy on galaxy, star on star,*
> *Planet on planet, asteroid on asteroid,*
> *Or even those four far walls of the sitting room . . .*

The final impression the poem leaves is of the tiny isolated self, lost in an unknowable universe, the same self that in 'Star-gazer' is set against a backdrop of cosmic immensity, the silence of the stars which terrifies us.

For the English Romantic poets this sense of individual isolation which dominates MacNeice's poetry was partly solved by belief in the benign influence of Nature, that goddess who 'ne'er deserts the wise and pure'. For modern man, who has sensed Nature red in tooth and claw in the grim Darwinian system, and who feels himself remote from natural landscape, Nature is an indifferent, sometimes cruel deity. This sense finds frequent expression in MacNeice's poetry. For the isolated self there is no simple solution in communion with Nature, for that goddess is suspected of cold, indifferent flashes of irrational cruelty. Mac-Neice would be sceptical of any simple Nature worship as a solution to the problem of value.

In *Mayfly* he counsels us sadly :

> *Nor put too much on the sympathy of things,*
> *The dregs of drink, the dried cups of flowers,*
> *The pathetic fallacy of the passing hours ...*

Morning Sun suggests that nature is 'merely dead' while *Iceland* is full of a sombre sense of the indifferent otherness of the landscape :

> *Night which began*
>   *Without device*
> *In ice and rocks,*
>   *No shade or shape;*
> *Grass and blood,*
>   *The strife of life,*
> *Were an interlude*
>   *Which must soon pass ...*

In *The Hebrides* the windows of the house open out on 'indifferent moors' and *Refugees* advises

> *But do not trust the sky, the blue that looks so candid*
> *Is non-committal, frigid as a harlot's eye ...*

whilst *Evening in Connecticut* clearly states that Nature is

> *Not to be trusted, no,*
> *Deaf at the best; she is only*
> *And always herself, Nature is only herself,*
> *Only the shadows longer and longer.*

Jigsaws (No. III) sees man as an iceberg jutting out of the sea of life, isolated and cut off from Nature by his intellect. There is a 'gulf between us and the brutes'. The last stanza sums up this separation from Nature, which paradoxically derives from what we share with the brutes :

> *Our lonely eminence derives*
> *From the submerged nine-tenths we share*
> *With all the rest who also run,*
> *Shuddering through the shuddering main.*

The isolated self in its 'lonely eminence' has, as well as alienation, to endure the certain knowledge of time's passage. MacNeice treats this common awareness with a dark, obsessive urgency that is particularly his own. Others have raged 'against the dying of the light', lamented with poignant delicacy the short lives of daffodils, or accepted mutability with pious resignation or stoicism, but few have written with the note of barely-controlled desperation that informs some of MacNeice's poems on time. In an early poem *Intimations of Mortality* (note the sceptical allusion) he tells of his fear of time when a child, in images of simple terror :

> *Then the final darkness for eight hours*
> *The murderous grin of toothy flowers,*
> *The tick of his pulse in the pillow, the sick*
> *Vertigo of falling in a fanged pit.*

This hectic passage of time is suggested most frequently in Mac-Neice's poetry by the trope of a journey by train or car. A poem representative of these is *Figure of Eight*, when understatement and prosaic diction create a sense of terror barely held in check :

> *But, winding up the black thread of his days,*
> *The wheels roll on and make it all too plain*
> *Who will be there to meet him at the station.*

In other instances MacNeice writes of the 'ages of man' (e.g. *The Tree of Guilt, The Slow Starter, The Habits*) suggesting the inevitable, relentless progression of time. The most powerful use of this trope is the short poem *Birthright* in which death is a horse that must be mounted :

> *I said 'To mount him means to die',*
> *They said 'Of course' . . .*

Life is minutes, hours and years when a man refuses to mount the deathly charger. But time gallops as the poem rollicks along with horrifying vigour, until the horse must be mounted. There is a note of frenzied terror in this poem, that can only be demonstrated by quotation, the swift rattle of the rhythm conveying the sense of the appalling rush of time :

> *The sun came up, my feet stuck fast,*
> *The minutes, hours, and years went past,*
> *More chances missed than I could count,*
> *The stable boys cried: 'Time to mount!'*
> *My jaw dropped and I gaped from drouth:*
> *My gift horse looked me in the mouth.*

The horror of age that comes upon a man unexpectedly is captured by MacNeice in a very fine late poem, *Soap Suds*. He has returned to a house of his childhood and the smell of soap as he is washing his hands reminds him of his past; he remembers playing croquet on the lawn. The association disturbingly presents him with the knowledge of age, the horrifying fact of his lost childhood :

> *And the grass has grown head-high and an angry voice*
> *cries Play!*
> *But the ball is lost and the mallet slipped long since from*
> *the hands*
> *Under the running tap that are not the hands of a child.*

The final image is very powerful.

The inevitability of time's passage means the inevitability of death. The train will come to the end of the line, the charger will have to be mounted, the 'rent is due'. Two of MacNeice's poems especially present this dominating awareness. In *Death of an Old Lady* an old lady

> *sails*
> *Towards her own iceberg calm and slow . . .*

as surely and as inevitably as the Titanic sailed on to founder on its iceberg. The poem (written as a tribute to his own loved stepmother) has a stately haunting beauty, but moves in its slow dignity to the simple, prosaic, factual conclusion of its final line—death :

> *At eight in the evening the ship went down.*

The second poem is different in tone but no less specific in its confrontation of the inevitability of death. In *Charon* a bus moves through London to meet the grisly ferryman on the banks of the Thames. The poem is dark, disturbing. The irreversible process of life towards death is subtly conveyed by repetition:

> *We just jogged on, at each request*
> *Stop there was a crowd of aggressively vacant*
> *Faces, we just jogged on . . .*

So in MacNeice's poetry the isolated self haunted by Time's passage travels to meet the dark ferryman of death:

> *Your health, Master Yew. My bones are few*
> *And I fully admit my rent is due . . .*

This poet has the knowledge that

> *all our games are funeral games . . .*

and

> *The move is time's, the loss is ours.*

Such is the world of MacNeice's poetry; such is the vision he observes with his ironic, mistrustful, sceptical eyes. By nature and sensibility a 'misunderstood Romantic' his scepticism allows no creation of a Romantic dream world, only a nostalgia for the lost 'felt unity' of childhood. He senses the dereliction that the death of God and scepticism about religion have left, and is frequently bitter, satirical, critical, about the 'frayed' world of the city, and its artificial, automatic pseudo-life. He is sceptical of any simple political creed, while he sympathetically or satirically portrays the victims of our time. He senses the loss of true human communication, as he mistrusts language. He presents as one of his major awarenesses the isolation of the self, the total separation of man from his environment, our 'lonely eminence' as creatures of intellect, as he is sceptical of any sentimental communion with Nature; and he is aware, with disturbing honesty, of the harsh facts of time and death. The isolated self peering out at the 'frayed' world of other people and of objects, sceptical of anything to make sense of it or give it value, will one day come face to face with a closed wall in which there is no window. It is in such a world and with such a sensibility that the question is asked :

> *And when we clear away*
> *All this debris of day-to-day experience,*
> *What comes out to light, what is there of value*
> *Lasting from day to day?*

And the sceptic must admit in many poems that perhaps the answer is—nothing. There may be no adequate answer. Nihilism presents itself to the sceptic as a valid philosophical and emotional option. In *Autumn Journal* MacNeice admits, though he emotionally rejects, the rational attractiveness of nihilism, its seductive force :

> *I know that you think these phrases highfalutin*
> *And, when not happy, see no claim or use*
> *For staying alive; the quiet hands seduce*
> *Of the god who is god of nothing.*

An early poem *Cradle Song for Miriam* is expressive, however, of total nihilism in its fifth stanza :

> *The world like a cradle rises and falls*
> *On a wave of confetti and funerals*
> *And sordor and stinks and stupid faces*
> *And the deity making bored grimaces. . . .*

There is a nihilistic despair in the final line of *Perseus*

> *And one feels the earth going round and round the globe*
> *of the blackening mantle, a mad moth.*

while *Eclogue from Iceland* fears that we are

> *capable all of that compelling stare*
> *Stare which betrays the cosmic purposelessness*
> *The nightmare noise of the scythe upon the hone.*

The brutal, harsh rejection of all anodynes in *Bagpipe Music* is nihilistic, while the late poem, *Greyness is all*, is filled with nihilistic feeling. The poem alters Edgar's dictum to produce a dark irony, and the poet in despair senses that even the black of the world is not black enough to 'pray against', to give hope of a corresponding whiteness. All we can do is wait for some fate

> *Contrived by men . . .*
> *. . . .*
> *To black out all the worlds of men*
> *And demons too but even then*
> *Whether that black will not prove grey*
> *No one may wait around to say.*

This is cosmic nihilism, malignant and horrifying.

Closely related to the clear expression of nihilistic feeling in the poetry, MacNeice wrote many poems that express a simple, unalloyed terror and fear of the world. The everyday, familiar world suddenly becomes menacingly horrific. The only possible reaction is a primitive terror, or nausea. In an early poem (*Spring Voices*, 1933), at the end of a realistic description of spring, the poet advises :

> *Do not walk, these voices say, between the bucking clouds*
> *alone*
> *Or you may loiter into a suddenly howling crater, or fall,*
> *jerked back, garrotted by the sun.*

Some of his poems do 'loiter' into the horror of this crater where commonplace experience takes on the menace of nightmare. Elsewhere seemingly topographical poems have a suggestion of brooding horror over them, of something not quite expressed, but about to enter to disrupt the world of the poem. Such is *The Rest House*, a poem curiously suggestive of imminent, frightful but unknown danger. The effect is produced by the imagery but also by the stealthy muted tones of the simple diction and the subtle menace of the sibilants :

> *The hissing lamp had hypnotised the lizards*
> *That splayed their baby hands on the wired window*
> *. . . .*
> *And on the dark the voices of unknown children,*
> *So shrill they might be white, sifted and splintered . . .*

But the horror is not always left below the surface. As we read in *Letter from India*, in Europe we have

> *written off what looms behind*
> *The fragile fences of our mind,*
>
> . . . .
>
> *So cast up here this India jolts us*
> *Awake to what engrossed our sleep;*
> *This was the truth and now we see it,*
> *This was the horror—it is deep;*
> *The lid is off, the things that creep*
> *Down there are we, we were there always.*

The horror in reality is still there, to be feared. It can reveal itself as it does to the character in *Il Piccolo Rifiuto* who has a vision of unrelieved horror, in the bric à brac of the familiar world, in the midst of cultural dislocation:

> *his eyes*
> *Blinked as the jets dived on the jampot*
> *He had not ordered and harpy-wise*
> *The insect world grew breasts and talons*
> *And wogs and wops kept babbling and mad*
> *Children went on a spacelark and God*
> *Began to limp and deep in the bad*
> *Shrubbery shrubs that should be ever*
> *Green turned brown.*

The poem fascinates and repels. The world has been transmuted in a repulsive, eerie process, as it has in *The Introduction*:

> *Crawly crawly*
> *Went the twigs above their heads and beneath*
> *The grass beneath their feet the larvae*
> *Split themselves laughing.*

Experience changes suddenly from the drably familiar, into a higher gear of unsettling oddity. Like a blurred photograph focusing to reveal horror, the world of *The Pale Panther* fixes gruesomely in the mind:

> *The sun made a late and lamented*
> *Spring. Yellow teeth tore*
> *The ribs of my roof. The giraffe*
> *Necks of blind lamp posts bent*
> *To lick up turds and print.*
> *Beyond the electric fence*
> *One tiny tractor stalled.*

At other times, MacNeice the sceptic controls his fear in a pose of disdainful, sophisticated cynicism and irony. This response is not, I would suggest, at the centre of his poetic sensibility, but it does exist. It is a cultured, tired distaste, wittily but undeniably moving towards life-denial in a less explicit way than direct expressions of nihilism, but with just as much force. It is present in his rejection of sexual love in *Autumn Journal*:

> *And the train's rhythm becomes the* ad nauseum *repetition*
> *Of every tired aubade and maudlin madrigal,*
> *The faded airs of sexual attraction*
> *Wandering like dead leaves along a warehouse wall.*

It reveals itself in such statements as:

> *That Man is a dancer is an anachronism—*
> *Who has forgotten his steps or hardly learnt them yet. . . .*
> > *(Precursors)*

and in a poem like *Hiatus*. This poem in dismissive tone treats of the futility of the war years:

> *a long way to fetch*
> *People to prove that civilisation is vain . . .*

The mood flashes momentarily in *Cock o' the North* in the brutality of the allusion:

> *Whose name was writ in bilge . . .*

and the bored disillusion of some of the passages in *Autumn Sequel*.

This mood of cynicism is not something that can be demonstrated conclusively by quotation. It is rather an atmosphere that envelops some of the poetry; it is a settled, evasive watchfulness which suggests that nothing may in fact be worthwhile because we do not have complete proof that anything is. It comes to us in guarded statement and plain expression, which refuses to be tempted by flights of emotion, reminding us that the poet was brought up to say no rather than yes unless the facts clearly demanded affirmation.

The English Romantic poets met the challenge of the drab, dehumanised Newtonian universe, the world which we have partly inherited, by a movement inwards. The world could be re-created by the power of the imagination, and the unpleasant, sordid, meaningless, material world dismissed or ignored. Mac-Neice, in some of his poetry, seems to be aware of this solution to the problem of meaning and value. Perhaps nihilism and cynicism can be avoided. One may reject the real world and live in the imagination. A late poem, *Flower Show* (1961), suggests this. It presents a visitor to a flower show who has overstayed the closing time. He is caught at night in a terrifying reality. The poet suggests that his eyes be bandaged (thus blotting out the real world) since 'now there is no way out', except in the world of the imagination, the world seen by inner vision. The poem ends:

> his inturned eyes before he falls may show him
> Some nettled orchard, tousled hedge, some garden even
> Where flowers, whether they boast or insinuate, whisper
> or shout,
> Still speak a living language.

Instead of the horrifying synthetic flowers of the darkened tent of the flower show (the outside world), the mind and the imagination may, when they have blotted out the world, contemplate a garden where flowers speak meaningfully ('a living language'). But this is hardly the triumphant self-assured faith of a Blake. There is a troubled hesitancy in the word 'may'. The Romantic way out may be 'no way out', either. The poem of course is ironical, for to bandage the eyes, to blot out the real world, is to risk a fall. So is pictured Romantic self-deception.

Blake at the height of his subjective ecstasy saw angels praising God, the character in *Flower Show* may have a vision of the perfect garden, but others looking inward, into the world of their subjectivity have visions as horrible as that seen by the character in *After the Crash*. The inner world may not be a world of beauty, value and meaning. It may be one of horror as it is to the girl in *Schizophrene*. In this poem events in the real world provoke imaginative journeys into the depths of the self, and although travelling into the countries of subjectivity may reveal green lands, or

> *fermenting rivers,*
> *Intricacies of gloom and glint,*

in this case the journey is

> *To a cold desert where the wind has dropped*
> *And the earth's movement stopped and something steals*
> *Up from the grit through nerve and bone and vein*
> *To flaunt its iron tendrils in her brain.*

If it were possible to reject the real world completely, some might live in a paradise of the imagination; others would live in hell. But it is not possible.[25] MacNeice is sceptical of this solution, as of all other simple anodynes. There can be only Romantic longing; there is no Romantic solution. The death of God, and with it of belief in a transcendent reality has robbed us of belief in our visions. The vision seen briefly in *Flower Show*, granted to the blindfold seer, is as unbalanced, as schizophrenic, as that seen by the girl in *Schizophrene*, no more, nor any less, a guide to the nature of reality.

For MacNeice, however, the real world, even for those who might dream delightfully, has an inconsiderate tendency to infringe on our reveries. There can be no escape from the actual world of tangible facts, objects and events. So the poignant, lyrical *Cradle Song for Eleanor* counsels Eleanor to seek peace and rest in

> *the only heaven,*
> *The robbers' cave of sleep.*

for

> *Life will tap the window*
> *Only too soon again . . .*

In sleep alone can the real world be escaped, and upon waking, life will encroach through the window (note the image) unbidden and unforbiddable. In *The Ear* the poet admits the impossibility of living completely in one's own subjectivity. There will always be sounds from outside, and we cannot decide which we shall admit. 'The choice/Of callers is not ours.' Although

We should like to be alone in a deaf hollow
Cocoon of self where no person or thing would speak . . .

away from the harsh unpleasantness of reality, 'In fact we lie and listen . . .' to such ordinary things as

the terrible drone of a cockchafer, or the bleak
Oracle of a barking dog.

The self may be alienated from the world, but there can be no escape from the duality in a satisfying subjective idealism.

This tendency for the real world to infringe upon us is wittily presented in another poem, *Flight of the Heart*. Here the poet, in response to the demands of the real world, declares that he will construct for himself a copper tower (ivory, perhaps, being in short supply) without access. A voice enquires (his alter ego?) what will he do when the tower shakes and falls. He replies that he will descend even further into his subjective world: 'I would go in the cellar and drink the dark'. But the voice asks him what he will do when the roof caves in, and he replies that he will return to a pre-human state:

I will go back where I belong
In the fore-being of mankind.

It is instructive to compare this poem with a poem by Dylan Thomas. In *Ears in the Turrets* Thomas uses the same image to suggest the world of subjectivity—the locked tower with no way in. But Thomas's is a quiet reflective poem, in which he contemplates whether the outside world should be admitted. He is able to meditate

Shall I unbolt or stay
Alone till the day I die . . .[26]

MacNeice's poem has a note of urgency, if wittily expressed. The attacks of the outside world are attacks—

Three sharp taps and one big bang . . .

—rather than the quiet grumbling of hands and fingers on the locks of the tower. MacNeice's poem ends with the tower and

F

cellar collapsed. Thomas is still pondering as his poem concludes. For Thomas, imagination's conflict with reality is an undecided contest. For MacNeice it is a foregone conclusion. The real world will always triumph. The sense that Yeats expressed in one of his earlier poems—

> *The cry of a child by the roadway, the creak of a lumber-*
> *ing cart,*
> *The heavy steps of the ploughman, splashing the wintry*
> *mould,*
> *Are wronging your image that blossoms a rose in the*
> *deeps of my heart . . .*[27]

—is a settled conviction in MacNeice's poetry. He is sceptical of any other viewpoint.

Thus the Romantics' solution is rejected in MacNeice's poetry, not because the poet is not tempted by their answers, but because he simply does not believe that the real, objective world can be re-created or dismissed so easily. The vision blossoming like a rose in the depths of the heart, even if we could believe in its validity, will always be interrupted by the coarse creaking of a lumbering country wagon, by the crass ugliness of the world, the incredible folly of men.

This flawed, 'frayed', valueless world that MacNeice senses, a world that cannot be escaped by indulgence in romantic reverie or escape into subjectivity, does not always draw from the poet a reaction of disgust and nausea, bored cynicism, and nihilistic dismissal. It sometimes evokes a proud stoicism. Life may be an immense waste, the world a valueless desert, but we can be men. This stoicism, akin to that of Matthew Arnold, finds expression in *Eclogue from Iceland* which, in the face of coming catastrophe in Europe, asserts :

> *Minute your gesture but it must be made—*
> *Your hazard, your act of defiance and hymn of hate,*
> *Hatred of hatred, assertion of human values,*
> *Which is now your only duty.*

MacNeice's moods of stoicism however are rather more positive than Arnold's. In Arnold one senses that the battle has been lost already and that the only expedient is to go down fighting gamely. In MacNeice's poetry the battle is going very badly, the world seems valueless, but the stoical affirmation of many may turn the tide against defeat. In this way MacNeice's stoicism is always about to move beyond itself, to become an affirmation of life and of value in life. *Explorations* considers the ordered, patterned, purposeful lives of the animal creation, and assesses our dissimilarities as a unique and 'despairing creature'. We can learn nothing of our purpose 'from whale or birds or worms'. The poem ends on a stoical note:

> *Our end is our own to be won by our own endeavour*
> *And held on our own terms.*

which is more than a last ditch stand, rather a counter-attack and consolidation. MacNeice's last poem is a poem in this stoical mood. It is an order to set sail, to put out to sea in defiance of all the adverse forces that converge on man. In knowing and facing the worst, man can still affirm the value of life in stoical action and effort.

> *Run up the sail, my heartsick comrades;*
> *Let each horizon tilt and lurch—*
> *You know your worst: your wills are fickle,*
> *Your values blurred, your hearts impure*
> *And your past life a ruined church—*
> *But let your poison be your cure.*

This is a very moving poem. It has obvious affinities with Tennyson's *Ulysses*, but the differences are worth noting. Where Tennyson's poem (perhaps intentionally, for it is after all a dramatic monologue) is inflated and windily rhetorical (suggesting a basic insecurity in the speaker's mind) *Thalassa* is terse, almost without sentimentality. Professor E. R. Dodds has written truly of the poem: 'With its stoical reaffirmation of his underlying faith in life it makes a fitting conclusion to his life's work.'[28]

3

Sceptical Faith

FOR the transcendentalist, (Christian, Idealist, or Platonist), the question of meaning and value is easily answered.[1] This world is not the only world; it may even be a mere shadow or appearance of the true, the real, which is elsewhere. Thus, true value may lie elsewhere, but certainly the present world of sense data is not the only one, and receives such value as it has from the other transcendent world. MacNeice, in his poetry, soundly and repeatedly repudiates a simple acceptance of such a view. Though he sometimes courts it as a possibility, as in the fifth poem of *Jigsaws* where he momentarily admits the need for a God to give value, his normal attitude is sceptically anti-transcendentalist. It is the attitude determining the first part of *Dark Age Glosses* (on the Venerable Bede):

> *How can the world*
> *Or the non-world beyond harbour a bird?*
> *They close their eyes that smart from the wood-smoke:*
> > *how*
> *Can anyone even guess his whence and whither?*
> *This indoors flying makes it seem absurd,*
> *Although it itches and nags and flutters and yearns,*
> *To postulate any other life than now.*

It had not always been thus with him. In *The Strings are False* he tells of his philosophic preoccupations at Oxford which were unashamedly transcendentalist:

I wanted the world to be One, to be permanent, the incarnation of an absolute Idea (though the word 'Idea' is inadequate since this Idea must be as much superintellectual as God, if there were a God, would be superhuman) . . . My tutor, one of

Oxford's few remaining neo-Hegelians, maintained, in the face
of the pigeon-hole philosophy flourishing at Cambridge, that
neither logic nor ethics could be separated from metaphysics.
I found his attitude sympathetic since my instinct was to drag
in ultimate reality everywhere.[2]

This sympathy quickly disappeared, for his natural instinct, as we
see it revealed in the poetry, was to deny any system which
denigrated the world of fact, our world. So *Leaving Barra*
(1937) categorically tells us:

> *For all the religions are alien*
> *That allege that life is a fiction,*
> *And when we agree in denial*
> *The cock crows in the morning.*

Furthermore his prevailing scepticism helped him in a move
away from Idealism. Religious scepticism about the existence
of some kind of deity must almost inevitably lead to disbelief
in a *transcendent* value-giving reality. The death of God helps
the death of old-fashioned metaphysics.

MacNeice's distaste for traditional Idealist metaphysics is implicit in those of his poems in which he prefers Aristotelianism
to Platonism. He expressed such a preference with a witty relish
in *Autumn Journal*:

> *Good-bye the Platonic sieve of the Carnal Man*
> *But good-bye also Plato's philosophising . . .*
>
> *(Canto II)*

Later in the same poem he explains it. He would rather live in
the real world of error, possibility and chance:

> *I am glad that I have been left the third best bed*
> *And live in a world of error.*
> *His world of capital initials, of transcendent*
> *Ideas is too bleak . . .*
>
> *(Canto XII)*

He prefers Aristotle who concerns himself with the tangible, biological world:

Aristotle was better who watched the insect breed,
The natural world develop,
Stressing the function, scrapping the Form in Itself . . .
(Canto XII)

Aristotle did not contemplate the timeless idea of the horse, but he opted for

Taking the horse from the shelf and letting it gallop.

A gloss on such passages as these is provided in *The Strings are False*: 'The Form of the Good, the One, may be food or it may be dope but it stops the hunger of the waifs of Here and Now. Many people therefore are ready to plump for the One until the wind blows under the door of that supposedly sound-proof system—"But where" says the wind coldly, "where are the other eleven?" Aristotle, if only by contrast with Plato, appeared as the champion of the Other Eleven.'[3] Aristotle represented for MacNeice the winds of here and now. Life always interrupts to announce that the world we have before us may indeed be the only world:

There is always a wife or a boss or a dun or a client
Disturbing the air.
. . . .
So blow the bugles over the metaphysicians . . .
(Canto XIII)

Aristotle conquers Plato; with a bugle call the real and only world is admitted.[4] Common sense triumphs. The horse is real, living and galloping, the plant growing and bearing seed.

Yet although MacNeice sometimes attempts to present himself as a poet of common sense and sturdy rationalism, he also displays a keen sympathy with the tenets of philosophic Irrationalism. Even the poet's pursuit of metaphysics at Oxford was highly infected with Irrationalist assumptions, if we are to believe the account given in *The Strings are False*:

Metaphysics for me was not something cold and abstract; it was an account of reality; but an artistic account, not a scientific one. I did not believe that one system of philosophy was truer than another and thought that philosophers themselves were fools in so far as they fancied they were getting to the bottom of anything; on the contrary their work was always superstructure, largely a matter of phrases, and these phrases were employed not as the physicist employs them but as the poet employs them; the philosopher's job—to use our favourite word—was stylisation, building a symphony which would sanction his emotional reactions to the universe. When you boil them down they are all alike. I found it amusing to collate a sceptic like Hume with one of the downright idealists. Hume denies the latter's Universals but he brings them back with an 'as if'. That was just eighteenth-century good manners—there's no such thing as blue blood but the world must go on *as if* there was.[5]

Note the phrase 'emotional reactions to the universe' which reveals the pedigree of his thinking at the time, with its assumption that intuition, not reason, is the best guide to life. This attitude is present in poems written throughout MacNeice's career,[6] for

> *Our half-thought thoughts divide in sifted wisps*
> *Against the basic facts repatterned without pause . . .*
> > *(Train to Dublin)*

So in *Ode* he prays for his son :

> *And let him not falsify the world*
> *By taking it to pieces;*

> *The marriage of Cause and Effect, Form and Content*
> *Let him not part asunder.*
> *Wisdom for him in the time of tulips*
> *Monastic repose, martial élan . . .*

In a fine lyric he celebrates reason's limitations. If we could get the hang of the world entirely (the poem is named *Entirely*) we might have some assurance, but on the other hand we might be merely bored. Happily however, language (the tool of reason) cannot encapsulate the reality of the passing life around us :

> *And when we try to eavesdrop on the great*
> *Presences it is rarely*
> *That by a stroke of luck we can appropriate*
> *Even a phrase entirely.*

For in fact, as he states in *Plain Speaking,*

> *In the beginning and in the end the only decent*
> *Definition is tautology: man is man . . .*

The Cromlech explicitly announces a Bergsonian, vitalist dislike and scepticism of the intellect. The poem replies to the 'extractors and abstractors', who want to know 'what was the essence in the flask', with a coy wit :

> *That to dissect a given thing*
> *Unravelling its complexity*
> *Outrages its simplicity . . .*

In *Day of Renewal* the poet is particularly sceptical about the possibility of Science explaining the mystery of being itself :

> *My What and How science might understand*
> *But neither the first nor last page tells the story*
> *And that I am remains just that I am. . . .*

while *Autumn Sequel* frequently displays this anti-rational bias. The later poetry expresses this attitude often, as in the richly affirmative lyricism of *Donegal Triptych* or in the conversational ease of *Time for a Smoke* and in the relish obvious in *Variation on Heraclitus*, for a dynamic view of the world, and for a perpetual flux beyond the reach of rational comprehension :

> *No, whatever you say,*
> *Reappearance presumes disappearance, it may not be*
> *nice*
> *Or proper or easily analysed not to be static*
> *But none of your slide snide rules can catch what is sliding*
> *so fast . . .*

Irrationalism for MacNeice, however, could no more provide a fully satisfying answer to the question of value than could any other simple philosophy. His own outlook was basically much more complex.

For the believer in a transcendent reality, as I have already argued, an apparent lack of value in the world is no real problem. For the sceptical MacNeice, however, the imperfections and limitations of this world could not be dismissed as irrelevant in the light of perfection in another. The question of value in the imperfect world had to be solved in that imperfect world, or nowhere. Paradoxically MacNeice frequently viewed life's imperfections and limitations as being creative of value. The fact that a thing (a person, an object, a scene, a work of art, a life) is limited and in that sense imperfect, that it is always changing and therefore never reaching the stasis of perfection, in a sense gives it value. Of prime importance in this conception of life as limited and therefore valuable, is the stark fact of death. In an early poem (*Ode*) the poet declares his preference for the limitation of life as against the infinite of eternity :

> *This segment of His infinite extension*
> *Is all the God of Him for me.* . . .

and he remarks

> *I want a sufficient sample, the exact and framed*
> *Balance of definite masses, the islanded hour.*

Note the imagery here, and the sense of limitation it conveys. The next stanza presents a list of images all redolent with the sense of limitation, of a thing being what it is and no more, bounded by the nature of its being :

> *As I walk on the shore of the regular and rounded sea*
> *I would pray off from my son the love of that infinite*
> *Which is too greedy and too obvious; let his Absolute*
> *Like any four-walled house be put up decently.*

The sea is 'rounded' in comparison with the infinite sea, as a circle is limited by the length of its circumference, and a house by its four walls.

Images of this nature are fairly frequent in MacNeice's poetry. Perhaps the most effective is that of the Garden, bounded by walls of limitation, or of a scene bounded by the horizon. As he writes (again in *Ode*)

> *We always have the horizon*
> *Not to swim to but to see* . . .

It is the wall of limitation. The horizon is not to be crossed, but is a great circle round us, containing us, limiting us. *Autumn Sequel* meditates on this awareness. Canto III contains the following brief vision :

> *Once upon a time there was a garden*
> *And once within that garden stood a tree*
> *Whose fruit must ripen as its bark must harden*
>
> *To bear the carved initials of you and me;*
> *Cradle on cradle swings upon its boughs,*
> *Coffin on coffin skulks beneath its lee.*

Implicit in these lines is the suggestion of the walls of life's limits, the natural bounds of birth, maturity and decay. Within the garden of limitation value is incarnate :

> *A glimpse of golden breasts, a mat of hair*
> *Thrown back from the eyes; a naked arm in a ray*
> *Of sunlight plucks an apple. Because it is there.*

The moment is poised within its limitations, valuable because of them. So Canto V of the same poem states :

> *Enclosed by trees and lawn*
> *These walls enclose a meanwhile. Meanwhile we*
> *Are here, not There ...*

We live within high walls rendering life what it is, and excluding all it is not :

> *This is a room.*
> *Of living people. Nothing perhaps avails*
>
> *Against the sea like rock, like doomed men against doom.*

What is, sustained by its limitedness, is. It cannot be denied, as the fact that a love affair (such as that celebrated in *Autumn Sequel*) happened cannot. A love affair, suffering the imperfections and limits of all human and earthly things, in a paradoxical sense also achieves its value from them. The poet affirms in Canto XI of *Autumn Sequel*

> *We did not call*
> *On God or Time to free us; nor did we want a free*
>
> *Hand, nor would we imagine a world at all*
> *Outside our present chains. Nor did we know*
> *That heavens, however green in leaf or gold in fall,*
>
> *Are not for ever, and yet can be heavens even so.*

The heaven of love has its spring time and its autumn. The lovers would not have wished it otherwise; they do not seek anything more permanent than our mutable world. The facts of mutability, change, death, imperfection and limitation, create value; the fact that a life must end makes it valuable; that leaves must change and die makes trees speak with tongues of flame. In the limited duration of their own particular time, changing towards death they achieve value and transcend time. The very limitedness of a life gives it value.

Perhaps the poems that present most clearly this aspect of MacNeice's poetic thought are *Plurality* and *The Trolls. Plurality* is a piece of lucid if somewhat prosaic philosophical discussion. The poet attacks Parmenides who would

> *smother life for lack of air*
> *Precluding birth and death ...*

in his monistic system, destroying thereby the essential limitedness of existence in an ideal crystal perfection. The poet has equally short shrift for the 'modern monist' whose 'terror of confusion freezes the flowing stream' in a 'craving for supreme/Completeness'. In contrast to this MacNeice states his conviction that

> *a man is what it is because*
> *It is something that began and is not what it was,*
> *Yet is itself throughout, fluttering and unfurled,*
> *Not to be cancelled out ...*

Man for MacNeice in this poem is an 'entity a denial of all that is not it.' He is limited, bound by what he is at a particular moment in the face of all that he is not. As he is a being, he is a denial of the negative forces of non-being. His very limitdness at any moment is an assertion of value in the face of nihilism. Later in the poem he hints at the pregnant paradox that the kind of perfection he wants is a perfection of imperfection :

> *No, perfection means*
> *Something but must fall unless there intervenes*
> *Between that meaning and the matter it should fill*
> *Time's revolving hand that never can be still.*

The only kind of perfection we can hope to attain is

> *to what a bird can find within the frame*
> *Of momentary flight (the value will persist*
> *But as event the night sweeps it away in mist).*

Note the image of limit here, 'the frame/Of momentary flight'. The poem concludes in a celebration of the 'imperfections' and limitations of life conscious that, paradox though it is, imperfection is the strange perfection by which our lives achieve their value. The other poem, *The Trolls*, is a confrontation of the forces of destruction and death. The first section of the poem presents the trolls (an air-raid) on a romp of destruction, unleashing the forces of non-being. The second section meditates on the positive value that limitation enables existence to have. This is what non-being (personified by the trolls) is trying to destroy :

> *Than which not any could be found other*
> *And outside which is less than nothing—*
> *This, as they call it, life.*

The complex syntax suggests the positive limitedness of life's 'isness', as the sentence struggles to highlight the word 'life' itself. Being is limited by the fact that nothing other than itself can exist. From this derives its value.

Now it is vitally important to make it clear that to speak of limitation at all means we have a conception of the possibility of the illimitable. We cannot speak of limited being without a conception of illimitable nothingness. Limited being, when we consider the possibility of illimitable non-being becomes valuable like a fire on a dark night, like a spring in a wasteland. So what we have been studying so far is a complex conception, basically a dialectical view of life. The value of a fire at night depends on the coldness and dark, on the possibility of its negation. So with life itself. It is valuable in view of the possibility of utter negation, total non-being. We know that it will change, die, exist within limits. Its very limitedness, in view of the possibility of the illimitable emptiness which is non-life, renders it valuable. The third section of the poem reminds us that we think we lose something with death but also reminds us that were it not for death

> *we should have nothing to lose, existence*
> *Because unlimited would merely be existence*
> *Without incarnate value.*

Note it has 'incarnate value'—value actually present in life, value in the flesh, in the object, in the event of perceiving the object and acting upon it, in living itself. The fourth part of the poem continues the examination of limitation as a constituent of value. Here the emphasis is on the limitation that duration creates. I simply quote the poem, which is perfectly explicit in its discussion of the value which limited duration imparts. Things change and die and are thus made valuable.

> *Than which not any. Time*
> *Swings on the poles of death*
> *And the latitude and the longitude of life*
> *Are fixed by death, and the value*
> *Of every organism, act and moment*
> *Is, thanks to death, unique.*

It is significant again that the structure of the syntax high-lights the simple word 'Is' in a poem celebratory of limited being, of a being unique within the limits of change and duration.

Non-being, death, the illimitable, the unknown, permanence, are all possibilities which when considered convince us of the values of their opposites : being, life, limit, the known, change. These paired opposites form a dialectic which renders life valu-able. As we shall see in the following chapter, the imagery of MacNeice's poetry frequently embodies imaginatively this dia-lectical conception of life (for instance in the frequent images of the sea attacking the land) but sometimes MacNeice states it quite bluntly. In *Brother Fire*, he states of his experience in the London air-raids, where fire and destruction were rampant :

> *Thus were we weaned to knowledge of the Will*
> *That wills the natural world but wills us dead.*

The forces of non-being, for all their horror, in a strange paradox 'will the natural world', and though they will our death, death makes life valuable.[7] It is instructive that in the poem MacNeice addressed the fire as 'dialectician fire'. The fire is the image of

a fundamental dialectic which renders life valuable in the face
of possible negation. In an article written in 1943, MacNeice
wrote words which cast further interesting light on this poem and
upon the thought behind it. He describes the air-raids:

> I have noticed myself that to walk along a great shopping
> street (imagine something like Madison Avenue) on the morn-
> ing after a Blitz, far from being depressing is almost exhilarat-
> ing (this may shock you but many people share my experi-
> ence); every step that you take crunches on glass and the whole
> street is tinkling as the shop walkers stand in their windows
> and sweep the glass onto the pavement where luxury objects
> lie scattered among torn-up flagstones and drunken lamp-
> posts; maybe there is a crater in the middle of the street
> containing a private car with water up to the tops of the
> wheels. This is havoc, but it is not heartbreaking. . . .

He continues:

> All the same I know we should ask ourselves every so often
> whether, living in these conditions, we are still seeing straight.
> I find that I vacillate as to the answer; sometimes I say to
> myself, 'This is mere chaos, it makes no sense', and at other
> times I think 'Before I saw war-torn London I must have been
> spiritually colour blind.' There is plenty of degradation—the
> cheapness inevitable in a world that involves so much short-
> term propaganda—and plenty of squalor, but there is also an
> exultation and when I say that I do not mean anything in the
> nature of Rupert Brooke heroics or last ditch bravado, I mean
> something much bleaker and in one sense humbler, something
> like the feeling you get on top of a mountain on a cold grey
> day. T. S. Eliot in a poem spoke of 'the still point of the
> turning world'; perhaps it is still the point of the *crashing*
> world that England has now become aware of. There is, in
> some quarters, an understandable swing back to religion but
> the revival of religion (with its ordinary connotations) is some-
> thing that I neither expect or desire. What is being forced
> upon people is a revival of the religious sense. And after the
> hand to mouth ethics of nineteenth-century liberalism and the
> inverted and blinkered religion of Marxism and the sentiment-
> ality of the cynical Lost Generation—after all that, we need

all the senses we were born with; and one of those is the religious.'[8]

The havoc of the destructive trolls, of the mad dog fire impresses the poet with the value of incarnate existence. This is sceptical faith.

It can be seen from the foregoing that MacNeice hints in his poetry at a philosophical position which sees value in the fact of Being itself, attacked as it is by forces that threaten negation. He may be sceptical of all traditional metaphysical or religious answers to the problem of how life can be affirmed as valuable, but this scepticism does not always lead him into the nihilism which he sometimes courts. The sceptical MacNeice believes in no transcendent reality but rather in the possibility of non-existence. The value of life depends on the possibility of death. The land is valuable because of the eroding sea, a garden is valuable in view of the great waste outside. Value is found in the fact, in view of the non-fact. It is to be found in things themselves, not in any transcendent realm of Ideas or religious otherworld. Value depends on a dialectic, between life and death. We need no heaven to affirm our life. So in a passage in his book on W. B. Yeats MacNeice writes:

> When we talk about the value of anything, we tend to suppose a gulf between this abstracted value and the thing which is valuable. This seems to me wrong. When a rose hits me in the senses, it is the rose that hits me and not some value separable from the rose. Idealist philosophers in talking about their Absolutes and Universals have made them vulnerable by hypostatising them, whereas the only invulnerable Universal is one that is incarnate. We still tend to think that, because a thing is in time, its value can be only explained by an abstraction from the thing of some supposedly timeless qualities; this is to explain the thing away. That a rose withers is no disproof of the rose, which remains an absolute, its value inseparable from its existence (for existence is still existence, whether the tense is past or future).[9]

So nihilism can be avoided; life can be celebrated independently. The value of life is implicit in the fact of life, poised as it is in a tension with the real possibility that life might not exist at all. Thus in the early poem *Ode* in a prayer that his son will lose the love of the infinite, the poet continues :

> *Let him accumulate, corroborate while he may*
> *The blessedness of fact*
> *Which lives in the dancing atom and the breathing*
> *trees . . .*

Another early poem (*Leaving Barra*) expresses a longing for 'the knack of knowledge' and confesses that the poet has only an 'inkling'. It continues

> *Though some* facts *foster the inkling—*
> *The beauty of the moon and music,*
> *The routine courage of the worker,*
> *The gay endurance of women . . .*
>
> (Author's emphasis.)

It is these facts themselves, in their very undeniable reality, which foster the inkling that life itself has value independent of any other world. In a beautiful love poem in *Autumn Journal* (Canto XI) MacNeice defies the intellect with its cerebral no-saying, in a celebration of the simple, glorious fact of love in the world. (This ability to defy the intellect in a celebration of being is also clearly related to the strong streak of Irrationalism which we noted in MacNeice's poetic thinking. The heart has reasons of which the head knows nothing.)

> *It has been proved that men are automatons,*
> *Everything wrong has been proved. I will not bother*
> *Any more with proof;*
> *I see the future glinting with your presence*
> *Like moon on a slate roof,*
> *And my spirits rise again. It is October,*
> *The year-god dying on the destined pyre*
> *With all the colours of a scrambled sunset*
> *And all the funeral elegance of fire*
> *In the grey world to lie cocooned but shaping*
> *His gradual return;*
> *No one can stop the cycle;*
> *The grate is full of ash but fire will always burn.*

Present here are suggestions of limitation ('destined pyre', 'funeral elegance', 'cycle') but also of the incontrovertible existence of things in the natural processes of life, between the natural bounds of birth and death (birth is suggested by the word 'cocooned'). The fire of being cannot be put out by the darkness of non-being.

It must be understood that this value implicit in facts is not merely something man attributes to them. If value is merely something we attribute to facts then it is a solipsistic construct; value dies with us. MacNeice in the poetry rejects a simple solipsistic attitude in an affirmation of a much more complex relationship between man the perceiver of value, and the world. This is the theme of *Plant and Phantom,* a poetic meditation on the nature of man's relationship to his world. The poet evokes in lyrical imagery the sheer vigour of man's experienced life, but also reflects upon it. Man is a creature

> *Who cheats the pawky Fates*
> *By what he does, not is,*
> *By what he makes, imposing*
> *On flux an architectonic—*
> *Cone of marble, calyx of ice,*
> *Spandrel and buttress, iron*
> *Loops across the void,*
> *Stepping stones in the random.*

This accepts the logic of solipsism, suggesting that the only meaning, order or value there can be in the meaningless flux of existence is that which man can make in his own mind. A further stanza continues this solipsistic thinking in its suggestion that meaning is created by

> *Smuggling over the frontier*
> *Of fact a sense of value,*
> *Metabolism of death,*
> *Re-orchestration of world.*

The only value is that made by man. The final stanza however hints at something quite different, hints that the value we smuggle over the frontier into the realm of fact may actually be implicit in that realm. Value is not simply a solipsistic construct but an intuition of something beyond us, something implicit and incarnate in the world of fact :

G

> *Who felt with his hands in empty*
> *Air for the Word and did not*
> *Find it but felt the aura,*
> *Dew on the skin, could not forget it.*
> *Ever since has fumbled, intrigued,*
> *Clambered behind and beyond, and learnt*
> *Words of blessing and cursing, hoping*
> *To find in the end the Word Itself.*

We may not be smuggling contraband at all. Value may not be so scarce in the country of fact. *The Newsreel* more explicitly posits value as 'beyond' and yet implicit in fact. There are moments of intuition which may merely be memory intruding value upon facts, but may also be evidence

> *To give us hope that fact is a façade*
> *And that there is an organism behind*
> *Its brittle littleness, a rhythm and a meaning,*
> *Something half-conjectured and half-divined,*
> *Something to give way to and so find.*

The Cromlech deals specifically and wittily with the notion that there is something intrinsically valuable in the facts of the world. The poem begins by evoking the minutiae of existing matter—'trivia of froth and pollen'—and proceeds to address itself to the philosophers' ('extractors and abstractors') problem—

> *And what is Life apart from lives*
> *And where, apart from fact, the value.*

To which problem the poet replies that intellectual abstraction destroys the thing itself. Yet he proceeds beyond mere Irrationalism to state :

> *For essence is not merely core*
> *And each event implies the world,*
> *A centre needs periphery.*

The poet continues by flaunting his belief that

> *Appearance and appearances—*
> *In spite of the philosophers*
> *With their jejune dichotomies—*
> *Can be at times reality.*

This is in flat contradiction of such modern metaphysicians as F. H. Bradley, who would tell us that appearance can never be reality. Appearance *is* reality. Fact is value. The poem concludes with pointed, playful wit, arguing that the brute fact of an existent entity cannot be generalised away. Two lovers holding hands cannot be generalised into worthlessness ('Dare an abstraction steal a kiss?'). The two lovers sitting in the clover field have their own 'given glory'—an intrinsic, implicit value. Nothing can disprove their love

> *Which is as sure intact a fact . . .*

as the cromlech with which the poem began. Value cannot be denied, even if field and lovers disappear.

This discovery that facts have their own undeniable, stubborn value, finds constant expression at all stages in MacNeice's poetry. He rarely presents the simple solipsistic solution to the problem of value, but rather the much more complex paradox that we create value by perceiving it, but that the thing perceived is also implicitly valuable in view of the possibility of negation, death, non-being. So MacNeice celebrates in many poems the rich fecundity of existence, in the face of the claims of nihilism. It is as if the very fact of being is value enough. For

> *dream was dream and love was love and what*
> *Happened happened—even if the judge said*
> *It should have been otherwise—and glitter glitters*
> *And I am I although the dead are dead.*
>
> *(Plain Speaking)*

This faith in the value of being itself is conveyed very beautifully in the poem *The Return* which tells of the passing of the old value-giving philosophies and religions, but affirms a belief in the sheer vigour of an existence that brings intrinsic value with it, in the very teeth of intellectual scepticism :

> *The harlequinade of water through a sluice,*
> *Tigers in the air, and in the teeth of science*
>
> *The acclamation of earth's returning daughter,*
> *Jonquils out of hell, and after*
> *Hell the imperative of joy, the dancing*
> *Fusillade of sunlight on the water.*

The departure of the old religions, of the old gods, has left the earth a heaven which we mistakenly assume to be a hell. Wallace Stevens in one poem told us that the death of one god is the death of all and questioned whether as a result our blood would fail, or would it come to be the blood of paradise. In this poem our blood does not fail. Earth itself is paradise. *Prospect* despite its comprehension of the horror of our 'frayed' world which could lead to despair, concludes with firm faith :

> *And though to-day is arid,*
> *We know—and knowing bless—*
> *That rooted in futurity*
> *There is a plant of tenderness.*

It is in this context of thought that MacNeice's celebration of people and love must be seen. The existence of people like Gwilym and Gavin (in *Autumn Sequel*) and the Casualty (see the poem *The Casualty*) and of love (like that celebrated with a moving lyricism in *Flowers in the Interval*) are a confounding of the god of nothingness who seduces with quiet fingers. These people are, love is, and nothing can deny that they exist.

All existent things, whether emotions, people, or objects, all can be valuable in and of themselves through their tangible stubborn factualness within the limitedness of their being. A late poem, *Indian Village*, states this specifically :

> *Whatever it is that jigs and gleams—*
> . . . .
> *Might yet prove heaven this side heaven*
>
> *Viz. life.*

The vigorous tangible reality of objects in the flux before us needs no heaven to endow it with value. It is its own kind of heaven.

The poetry throughout captures and expresses this incontrovertibly existent reality of a fecund nature. The world of external nature, of vital objects, frequently appears in the poetry as a world of vigorous, undeniable activity. A consideration of some of the words MacNeice uses to describe natural events is instructive. Vegetables contain 'roaring sap', a sound is 'like stigmata', while the activity of Nature is frequently presented by use of verbs of vigorous action. Plants 'toss their trumpets' (*The King-*

dom), the edges of roads are 'foaming white' (*The Stygian Banks*) a sky of peach 'explodes its pulp' (*Autumn Sequel*), green shoots in December come 'stabbing upwards' (*Autumn Sequel*), bogland streams 'prowl and plunge' (*Donegal Triptych*), a trout stream will 'chirp and gurgle' (*Donegal Triptych*), coffee 'leaps', 'chugs' and 'glints while birds gossip' (*Country Weekend*) and tulips 'tug at their roots' (*Another Cold May*).

This quality of vigorous, tangible objective reality in the world, external to the poet, is captured in poem after poem in stanzas such as this from *The Park* :

> *Through a glass greenly men as trees walking*
> *Led by their dogs, trees as torrents*
> *Loosed by the thaw, tulips as shriekmarks*
> *(Yelps of delight), lovers as coracles*
> *Riding the rapids: Spring as a spring*
> *Releasing the jack-in-a-box of a fanfare.*

It is this very quality that convinces the isolated subjectivity (obsessed with itself and its sense of nihilism) of the existence of an external valuable reality of objects, people and their emotions.

> *The Self finds itself in predestined*
> *Freedom. Around, below, above,*
> *Glinting fish and piping birds*
> *Deny that earth and truth are only*
> *Earth, respectively, and words.*

> (*Vistas*)

The external world breaks into the self, forces its way through the barriers, presenting its own vital value of tangible immediacy to the doubting, sceptical sensibility. MacNeice's poems announce how impossible it is for the self to concern itself only with subjective experience. The isolated, lonely, cogitating, fearful self will never be allowed to remain in that condition without alleviation. Reality with its own inherent value is always there, ready to impinge (even if undesired by the subjective Romantic escapist) on the consciousness, ready to break the window, to convince of the value of experience, defeating nihilism which threatens to seduce the intellect. An opening rose cannot be denied and new experiences of things outside and beyond us are continually surprising us :

For every static world that you or I impose
Upon the real one must crack at times and new
Patterns from new disorders open like a rose
And old assumptions yield to new sensation . . .

(*Mutations*)

The awareness that reality will always impinge on the self with
its own tangible value of immediacy and vigour is present in
MacNeice's poetry in two ways. Firstly, many poems are organised in a manner which suggests it. Secondly, a number of poems
state this idea specifically. First the organisation of the poetry.

Frequently MacNeice's poetry is meditative, often pondering
problems of metaphysics or politics or religion. Often, however,
the meditative verse is interrupted by a sudden sense of the
vigour of nature, of the reality of the outside world. A meditative,
subjective poem will suddenly become celebrative or descriptive
of the natural world. It is as if the world has suddenly impinged
itself on the introspective, meditative consciousness of the poet.
For example, after a long thoughtful passage in *Autumn Sequel*
(Canto III) we suddenly come upon :

The mild September evening blows a kiss
In ripples over the lake, a sky of peach
Explodes its pulp . . .

Meditation, followed by description or celebration of external
reality, is repeated many times through this work and in the
poetry in general. *London Rain* for example—a consideration of
the possible existence of God—continues thoughtfully for nine
stanzas. The poem is suddenly broken into by a tenth stanza
which presents the immediate world of tangible reality :

So let the water sizzle
Upon the gleaming slates,
There will be sunshine after
When the rain abates . . .

It is as if the world suddenly swims into view asserting its own
'blazing truth' (the phrase is from *Autumn Sequel*), affirming
the value of simple, tangible existence and answering the doubts
and questions, the sceptical cerebration of the conscious self,
by making them seem somehow irrelevant in the face of such

undeniable 'isness'. The structure of the poem (meditation/ celebration) suggests this.

Secondly, there are a number of poems which describe directly the occurrence of this valuable encroachment of the real world upon the self. An early poem *Snow* describes just such an occasion, with a zestful tang. The poet looking out of the window (note my earlier discussion of this imagery) sees 'snow and pink roses against it'. They are 'soundlessly collateral and incompatible', each existing as a separate positive entity, distinct, separate and valuable in their limited particularity. The world

> *is crazier and more of it than we think,*
> *Incorrigibly plural.*

As we read in *Plurality*,

> *world is full of blind*
> *Gulfs across the flat, jags against the mind,*
> *Swollen or diminished according to the dice,*
> *Foaming, never finished, never the same twice.*

This drunkenness of variety, of particular objects and events, pierces the window of separation and forces a sense of value on the isolated consciousness.[10] Thus isolation is broken down.

The experience of objects and people impinging upon the self is frequently suggested in MacNeice's poetry by the trope (as in *Snow*) of an appearance beyond glass or a window. So in *Slow Movement*

> *Great white nebulae lurch against the window*
> *To deploy across the valley . . .*

and in *The Revenant*

> *The windows of our life were placed*
> *So that their panes were blurred with breath.*

Late poems like *Windowscape* and *The Park* (where the self forces its way out through the grille of a window 'to find the world') employ it, while specific use of the trope is the long poem of mid-career, *The Window*. This poem begins by contrasting a painting, a window on a static world of perfection, with our own life—looking out through a window on flux, change and imperfection. Because of this window, the self is a 'never private pool'. Faces, objects, voices, sounds, force their way in through the window, swim before the glass, and sometimes they are

> *All looking in and their eyes meet yours, the hour-glass*
> *turns over and lies level* ...

and in some mysterious way

> *we lose ourselves*
> *In finding a world outside.*

The self-existent undeniable being of reality itself quietens the doubts of the sceptical, subjective self. The curse of self-conscious-ness is lifted in a kind of mystic identification and communion with the external,[10] which transcends both subject and object:

> *our lives transcended*
> *While and because we live.*

In this knowledge, that such a communion is possible, the poet can take everything on trust and look out through his window

> *to where others*
> *Look out at him, be proudly humbled*
> *And jettison his doubt.*

The affirmation can be made, and in certain poems MacNeice manages to make it. It is an affirmation not dependent on any traditional metaphysical, imaginative, political or religious system, of which MacNeice would be sceptical. It is dependent, rather, on the simple existence of things and people themselves, limited as they are, attacked by death as they are. It is the sceptic's faith.

PART II

Techniques and Strategies

Poetry you think is only the surface vanity,
The painted nails, the hips narrowed by fashion,
The hooks and eyes of words; but it is not that only,
And it is not only the curer sitting by the wayside,
Phials on his trestle, his palms grown thin as wafers
With blessing the anonymous heads;
And poetry is not only the bridging of two-banked rivers.

(Eclogue by a Five-barred Gate)

4

The Poet and his Imagery

THERE are at least two kinds of study of a writer's imagery. First, there is the mere statistical classification of imagery, which tells us that a poet uses the image of the Madonna (or what have you) so many times. This is a necessary precursor to the second kind of study, but if it is not carried any further it seems to me a rather futile exercise. The second kind of study is more complex, for out of the statistical observations it sees patterns developing. It sees that certain ideas are consistently pictured, given poetic expression, by particular images or groups of images. This is in no way to suggest that the poet has ideas which he decorates with the icing of imagery. It is rather, that within the composite world of the poetry, internal, sometimes private significances are created. For the imagery which a poet habitually employs, creates a cosmos, a poetic universe, a landscape of the imagination which we are permitted to enter, a landscape redolent with significance internally created and sustained. On the authority of Robin Skelton we know that MacNeice himself thought of poetry in this way, thought that the poet re-creates in poetry his private imaginative universe. Skelton in a book on poetry cites MacNeice as follows: 'Indeed, Louis MacNeice has said that, in his opinion, each poet has a mental "country" to which his poems belong',[1] and 'Louis MacNeice suggests that this country is almost totally that of childhood experience; its symbolic natural features are things which deeply affected the poet as a child.'[2] Whether a poet's poetic landscape always originates in childhood experience is debatable[3] (though I consider it likely, and it certainly seems the case with MacNeice). It is true, however, that in any poetry we are introduced to a 'mental' imaginative country.[4] The task of the second kind of image study is to explore the geography of this 'country'. To this, the exploration of the imaginative world of MacNeice's poetry, we shall now turn.

A central motif in the world's literature is the journey. It is the basis of the Greek epics. It is present in Beowulf, in Malory, in Langland, in Chaucer, Spenser, Bunyan and in the poetry of the great Romantics. MacNeice himself has written on the prevalence of this motif in world literature. He wrote 'Such a voyage, like any form of quest, has an immemorial place in legend. And the theme crops up again and again in sophisticated literature : look at *The Ancient Mariner*. The great majority of folk tales include journeys, sometimes on sea, more often on land, and the quest which in such stories is usually aimed at finding a fortune or a bride can become in other hands the Quest of the Grail or the City of Zion.'[5] It is a frequent motif in Mac-Neice's poetry.

In many of MacNeice's poems imagery of quest is explicit. In others it is present in related concepts. Such imagery in Mac-Neice's poetry is usually associated with the poet's conviction that man must create value in the world by his own effort, knowing that although 'The world is what is given. . . . we only can discover/Life in the life we make'. The image of the quest clearly expresses this. It is an image of the sceptic's determination to make something of a world he senses can be made valuable in no other way.

The most explicit linkage in the poetry,[6] of quest imagery with a celebration of the value of action, is found in *The Stygian Banks* :

> *Let the blossom*
> *Fall, that is fact but the fact can be retranslated*
> *To value of blossom and also to value of fall;*
> *While we, who recognise both, must turn our backs on*
> *the orchard*
> *To follow the road of facts which we make ourselves*
> *Where others, men, will help us to conjure value*
> *In passing and out of passing but always turning*
> *Our backs on the road we have made*
> *Until—which has value too—at a certain point we fall*
> *And the hoop topples into the ditch. The well-worn*
> *symbols*
> *Of quests and inns and pilgrims' progresses*
> *Do correspond; the inn-sign clanks in the night . . .*

while one of the central images of affirmation in *Autumn Sequel* is the questlike journey of the Magi. In a late poem of lyrical celebration in the face of nihilistic denial, the imagery is of quest and attainment:

> *And when the last horn burns the hills*
> *Fetch me far one draught of grace*
> *To quench my thirst before it kills.*

> (*Invocation*)

This is the world of *The Dark Tower* and of Browning's strange landscape in *Childe Roland*.

> *And yet*
> *Dauntless the slung horn to my lips I set*
> *And ble*w. 'Childe Roland to the Dark Tower Came'

Often, however, the use of the imagery of quest is not so explicit, but is no less present. Allusions to such figures as St Brendan and Sir Patrick Spens are examples of this implicit use, as is a poem such as *Sailing Orders* which suggests that 'beliefs are still to make' in the trope of setting out on a journey over the sea. A similar poem is the last in the *Collected Poems* (1966): *Thalassa*, where we are urged anew to the quest:

> *Put out to sea, ignoble comrades,*
> *Whose record shall be noble yet ...*

The quest is suggested in lines such as these from *Eclogue from Iceland*:

> *do not avoid the ambush,*
> *Take sly detours, but ride the pass direct.*
> *But the points of axes shine from the scrub, the odds*
> *Are dead against us. There are the lures of women*
> *Who, half alive, invite to a fuller life*
> *And never loving would be loved by others.*

Here is the quest Hero's fear of corruption, his testing, and his temptations.

Imagery drawn from the tale of the Sleeping Beauty is associated with these images of quest in the poet's mind. In a beautiful passage of *Autumn Journal* (Canto XI) the poet treats a love affair in imagery of the quest/romance:

> *And then of a sudden I see her sleeping gently*
> *Inaccessible in a sleeping wood*
> *But thorns and thorns around her*
> *And the cries of the night*
> *And I have no knife or axe to hack my passage*
> *Back to the lost delight.*

In *Woods*, longing for romantic love is expressed in terms of fairy romance, suggestive of the sleeping beauty, while in *Letter from India* he writes to Hedli MacNeice:

> *the crickets*
> *Plait a dense hedge between us so*
> *That your voice rings of long ago,*
> *Beauty asleep in a Grimm story.*

The questing prince must break down the hedge of separation to achieve love. A beautiful use of this imagery to evoke the quest for the value of love is the first poem of *Flowers in the Interval*:

> *Without you once, in the wilderness, pondering years*
>   *and years,*
> *I heard thin strings in the air, came round a corner*
> *On a quickset hedge of fiddlebows and my ears*
> *Tingled because I was thinking of someone unknown*
>   *to me*
> *Who had pricked her finger and slept while the long*
>   *nights grew*
> *Into a tangle of quivering hands and gracenotes*
> *Through which I plunged and found her—and she was*
>   *you.*

The long, arduous quest is over.

At times the imagery of quest flickers only for a moment in specific reference. Writing of timeless moments (in poem two of *Visitations*) when

> *All things existent*
> *Grow suddenly dearer . . .*

the poet sees such experiences in terms of quest imagery:

And the grail next door,
Though the wind drop dead
And the threshold sentry
Forbid—let him tread
By the light in his core,
He still finds entry.

At other times such reference is implied by related imagery—
by imagery which suggests the unwavering dedication of the
Quest hero, or the temptations and testings he had to endure.
His testings are suggested by allusions to the dark woods and
forests of romance in which the questing knights of Malory
and Spenser found themselves:

the wood of our desires
Consists of single yet entangled trees
Which maybe form a wood the world requires

But yet a wood which none distinctly sees
Or fully finds his way in.

Yet we must try to find our way, and like questing heroes, escape
from the wood and make something of our experience. A
late poem, *Selva Oscura*, pictures this wood of quest romance,
where, on the journey the hero may suddenly come upon something, or someone, that will give value and meaning to life.
Perhaps, journeying like Dante through the perplexing, haunted
wood of oneself, the grail may be found. Stoically we must set
out and perhaps reach a destination.

Perhaps suddenly too I strike a clearing and see
Some unknown house—or was it mine?—but now
It welcomes whom I miss in welcoming me;
The door swings open and a hand
Beckons to all the life my days allow.

But a journey is not always a quest, and in MacNeice's poetry
life is often imagined as a journey whose destination is ambiguous. In a very early poem, *Happy Families* (1928), the poet
considers a family *diaspora*:

John caught the bus, Joshua caught the train,
And I took a taxi, so we all got somewhere . . .

while another early poem (*Breaking Webs*) employs a car journey
as a trope of life. *Train to Dublin* presents the poet on a train
journey, while in the third poem of *Trilogy for X* the image's
significance is defined :

> *From the moving train of time the*
> *Fields move backwards.*

In *Autumn Journal*, the evanescent pleasures which early
married life offered in Birmingham provoke imagery of the train
journey :

> *We slept in linen, we cooked with wine,*
> *We paid in cash and took no notice*
> *Of how the train ran down the line . . .*
>
> (*Canto VIII*)

As we have suggested MacNeice is keenly aware of the perpetual flux which is the world, and experience. The train
image is a perfect expression of this, for it suggests a rapid
movement through a world of vanishing particulars where
new data or phenomena present themselves continually. The
landscape outside our window is never static. We observe
but lack time to comprehend, as a scene glimpsed from a
carriage window is gone before we have time to think about it.
The image has a peculiar ambiguity which is part of its potency,
for in life, as in a train, it is impossible to tell whether it is we
who are moving, or whether it is the outside world of experience
and objects. Do things disappear because we travel on towards
death, or do they move backwards away from us? Are we
stationary or are they? Is it a matter of

> *It is we who pass them—hours of stone*
> *Long rows of granite sphinxes looking on . . .*

or

> *Time's face is not stone or still his wings?*

The trope of a train journey maintains the irresolvable tension
between subject and object that we noticed as one of Mac-
Neice's themes in the previous chapter.

Little would be gained by examining all the poems in which
specific use is made of train images.[7] It would be more instructive

to mention MacNeice's frequent use of associated imagery. Obviously images of car or boat journeys are of the same type. These occur with an almost equal frequency, as in *The Wiper* or *The Atlantic Tunnel*. In *Autumn Journal* is another variant:

> *And so to London and down the ever-moving*
> *Stairs . . .*
>
> (*Canto I*)

and in *Autumn Sequel* we encounter this image again:

> *the moving stairs*
> *Move up and down crowded with empty shoes . . .*

Later in the same poem the imagery of a journey and that of the moving staircase are linked. A new day is seen as

> *one further day*
> *Of traffic lights to count, of moving stairs*
> *To move on . . .*

Also associated with these images of the journey of life in time, is the image of the river. Life is a never (or almost never) ceasing river, bearing away the present experienced reality, substituting the new (or conversely bearing us away from experience to new experience). In *London Rain* the poet regards life as 'the living river', while *Donegal Triptych* is constructed around this conception. The trope of the river is less exact, less resonant as an image of man in the temporal process, than the train, bus or car imagery. Obviously there is not the same sense of man looking out at a world of swiftly changing objects. However, there is the same sense of perpetual motion and inevitable change.

Further associations with these imaginative conceptions, which suggest a life a perpetual change in time, are many which picture life and time as a thread or ball of wool constantly being wound out. There are few things more unredeemable than a neat ball of wool, unwound and deposited on the floor, in a knotted tangle. Life in time is wound out continually and cannot be untangled. So in *Cradle Song for Miriam*:

H

> *The clock's untiring fingers wind the wool of darkness*
> *And we all lie alone, having long outgrown our*
> *cradles ...*

In *Eclogue between the Motherless* character A declares

> *Like a ball of wool*
> *That kittens have got at, all my growing up*
> *All the disposed-of process of my past*
> *Unravelled on the floor ...*

while in *Autumn Journal* (in a passage in which the poet is discussing our constant anticipation of the morrow) he imagines the process of temporal succession thus :

> *the spider spinning out his reams*
> *Of colourless thread ...*

The sixth poem of *Novelettes* portrays a character ('The Preacher') whose life is 'Sixty years' expended thread . . .' while in *The News-Reel* the passage of time since Munich is

> *A tangle of black film*
> *Squirming like bait upon the floor of my mind ...*

—expended thread. The final sections of *Autumn Sequel* expand on this conception.

At times these images of trains, cars, rivers and thread are compressed into an image which contains two or more of them in an image cluster, so prevailing is MacNeice's sense of the passage of time. So in *Autumn Journal* the train, car and thread images are compressed :

> *And the rebels and the young*
> *Have taken the train to town or the two seater*
> *Unravelling rails or road*
> *Losing the thread deliberately behind them ...*

Sometimes, however, the journey is broken, the moving train stops; the stairs stop moving and the river ceases to flow. The poetry suggests an ambivalent attitude to this cessation. In *Meeting Point*, when someone stops the moving stair we are told :

> *The stream's music did not stop*
> *Flowing through heather ...*

implying that although the stairs and the stream stop dead, the moment is still a blessed one of communication in human love. The stream stops, but its music continues. *Slow Movement* presents a moment when:

> *The movement ends, the train has come to a stop*
> *In buttercup fields ...*

It has stopped for a moment of timeless beauty, as does the stream in *Donegal Triptych*.

> *It is good to pause on the turn, look back on the glittering*
> *silent spiral*
> *Of time in a timeless moment where the nether blue*
> *meets the upper blue.*

Yet in each of these instances it is assumed that the cessation of motion is not absolute. In *Meeting Point* the music of the stream can still be heard. In *Slow Movement*

> *what happens next on the programme we do not know ...*

but it is assumed that something will, surprises keep us going. In *Donegal Triptych*, the timeless moment of communion past, the river begins to flow again,[8] to bring new experiences and sights. Change prevails. There can be, however, another kind of cessation—petrification.

MacNeice, as we have seen, views change and the limitedness this implies as integral to the value of events, objects and experiences. Things must change to be valuable, the train must keep moving, the river must begin again after the timeless moment. Stasis is anathema. So a number of poems are based on the notion that the train can stop for ever. Their emotional content is one of distaste and fear. When the train stops finally, life is valueless. Numerous poems contain a real fear of petrification. This fear is expressed by a variety of images. They embody the poet's persistent fear of a 'complete fusion of subject and object; a full stop; death'.[9]

In an early poem, *Mayfly*, when the poet thinks of the tragic fact of death, his thought is embodied in imagery of stone:

> *hours of stone,*
> *Long rows of granite sphinxes looking on . . .*

while *Circe* is a horrified consideration of petrification:

> *This despair of crystal brilliance.*

In *The Glacier* the ever-revolving traffic (an image of time's speed) circulates with such persistence and velocity that

> *the whole stream of traffic seems to crawl*
> *Carrying its dead boulders down a glacier wall*
> *And we who have always been haunted by the fear of*
> *becoming stone*
> *Cannot bear to watch that catafalque creep down . . .*

Perseus of another poem (*Perseus*) enters a hall 'carrying a stone death' and a whole company freezes. So it is sometimes in our own experience. A friend enters, one suddenly feels dead, the pages of a book are 'leaden' and the hours are 'hooded and arrested'—the train has shuddered to a terrifying halt—petrification. In *Eclogue between the Motherless* the fear of a dead stop is suggested by a different but no less potent image cluster—a character considering his past remarks

> *Whom recording*
> *The night marked time, the dog at the lodge kept barking*
> *And as he barked the big cave opened of hell*
> *Where all their voices were one and stuck at a point*
> *Like a gramophone needle stuck on a notched record.*

The effective image of the needle stuck in a gramophone record occurs again in later poems. *The Heated Minute* expresses the same fear in imagery which suggests that the world has slowed down, has become ponderously stationary:

> *And the world piles high with ash . . .*

The neurotic woman in *Schizophrene* is also haunted by a fear of petrification, when in her mind

> *the scene shifts*
> *To a cold desert where the wind has dropped*
> *And the earth's movement stopped . . .*

while in *Plurality* petrification is once more imagined as a freezing of the flowing stream. *The Casualty* uses another image to suggest the petrification, which is death (metaphorically and literally), when the poet writes of Graham Shephard's[10] death that

> *the shutter fell*
> *Congealing the kaleidoscope at Now . . .*

This is a potent image, for there is nothing more dead, more suggestive of petrification, than a badly taken snapshot. The meaningful flux of life seems to be frozen into a dead, fatuous fixity. In *Autumn Sequel* fear of petrification is contained in the image of repeating clocks, while a similar image is used in *Half Truth from Cape Town*. Here the poet is haunted by

> *a calling dove,*
> *Its voice like a crazy clock that even ten*
> *Minutes runs down, so must be wound again . . .*

Hold-Up powerfully presents the poet's fear of petrification (it should be compared with *Figure of Eight*, another late poem, which presents a man in a train, terrified of reaching his destination where, it is implied, death may be waiting). In this poem the bus, the journey, comes to a dead, horrifying halt—all movement halts in a nauseating, fixed petrification :

> *The engine stalled, a tall glass box*
> *On the pavement held a corpse in pickle*
> *His ear still cocked, and no one spoke,*
> *No number rang, for miles behind*
> *The other buses nudged and blared*
> *And no-one dared get out. The conductress*
> *Was dark and lost, refused to change.*

We must keep moving, to keep living; to halt means horror and death, for the sceptical poet can only find value in a world of change.

A number of petrification images in MacNeice's poetry create a problem for the reader. Most of those noticed so far are quite comprehensible; they clearly suggest, embody, the idea of petrification and create the accompanying distaste or fear of it. Concept and emotion are equally explicit. The train coming to a halt, the clock winding down every ten minutes, the record stuck in a groove, the frozen stream—all these are meaningful to the reader and convey to him instantly, and usually with considerable poetic force, the idea intended. MacNeice, however, also uses the sound of church bells as an image of the fear of petrification, as suggestive of the horrifying halt, which means death. Yet for many people there is nothing even unpleasant in the sound of church bells. Some biographical details help us to interpret aright. In 'Experiences with Images' MacNeice tells us: 'My father being a clergyman, his church was a sort of annex to the home—but rather a haunted annex (it was an old church and there were several things in it which frightened me as a child). Which is one reason, I think, though I would also maintain that the sound is melancholy anyhow, why church bells have for me a sinister association . . .'[11] He tells us in another reminiscence that as a child he had always been afraid in the church: 'on my earliest visits to the church there were things in it that frightened me'.[12] He also wrote of the terrors of the church in the early pages of *The Strings are False*. He disliked church bells. In *Train to Dublin* he hears in a shell the sound of the sea which reminds of :

> the mere
> *Reiteration of integers, the bell*
> *That tolls and tolls, the montony of fear . . .*

suggesting both fear, and the repetition which is akin to petrification. In *Homage to Clichés* the poet is haunted by the horrifying silence of an eternal bell which does not deign to move :

> *Stoop your head, follow me through this door*
> *Up the belfry stair.*
> *What do you see in this gloom, this womb of* stone?
> *I see eight bells hanging alone.*
> *Eight black panthers, eight* silences
> *On the outer shell of which our fingers via hammers*
> *Rapping with an impertinent precision*
> *Have made believe that this was the final music.*
>
> (Author's emphases.)

Here is a clear association of bells with petrification. This becomes even more evident later in the poem :

Never is the Bell, Never is the Panther, Never is Rameses
Oh the cold stone *panic of Never—*
The ringers are taking off their coats, the panther
                                                    crouches
The granite *sceptre is very slightly inclining* . . .
                                    (Author's emphases.)

In the delightful, moving, lyric *The Sunlight on the Garden*, MacNeice writes:

The sky was good for flying
Defying the church bells
And every evil iron
Siren . . .

A knowledge of his biography is imperative, to catch the full import of the imagery. The beauty and free movement of flight defy the cold 'iron' petrification of the church bells. The woman of *Schizophrene* is haunted by the sound of church bells, which we are told

                                                    express
The claims of frozen Chaos and will clang
Till this and every other world shall melt
And Chaos be Itself and nothing felt.

Once again we note the association of the bells with fear and petrification ('frozen chaos'). A similar image cluster is found in Canto XVII of *Autumn Sequel* where stone and bells come together.

The church bells call
Forlornly from their cages within cages,
Oak beams within blind stone . . .

In a late poem, *Half Truth from Cape Town*, the poet tells us with dark despair 'The bell went on forever'. The danger of petrification, of death, of everything grinding to a halt is ever present, and we are reminded of it by the monotonous, continual clamour of the bells.

MacNeice, as we noted earlier, reveals in his poetry a preference for Aristotle, rather than Plato, because, as he puts it in 'When I was Twenty-one', 'Aristotle being among other things a zoologist, never let transcendental radiance destroy the shapes of the creatures or impose a white-out on everything.'[13] Aristotle left room for a world of limit, particularity and constant change (all integral to MacNeice's conception of value). Yet in the imagery of MacNeice's poetry, a sense of the possible existence of the eternal is still present. It is an eternity of transcendental radiance that could impose a white-out on everything. In some of the images of petrification that we have been discussing, there is a suggestion that the stasis he fears is that of the white fixity of the eternal. This is implied in the image of death as a final snap-shot, in the petrification imagery used in the philosophic poem *Plurality* to condemn the 'modern monist' who

> *evokes a dead ideal of white*
> *All-white Universal . . .*

and is particularly evident in the bell imagery. In *Homage to Clichés* the bell is described as 'the eternal bell' and

> *never is sometime*
> *Never is the bell . . .*

In *Schizophrene* the bell reminds of the possibility of the world melting 'And chaos be itself and nothing felt'.

In MacNeice's essay 'Experiences with Images' there is a passage vital to the understanding of his thought and its expression :

> I ought by rights to explain what as a poet I am getting at. But this is not so easy, as at different times I have been getting at different things and as at all times (like all poets?) I have been answering questions I was not fully aware of having asked. But I think that, generally speaking, my basic conception of life being dialectical (in the philosophic, not in the political sense), I have tended to swing to and fro between descriptive or physical images (which are 'correct' as far as they go) and *faute de mieux* metaphysical, mythical or mystical images (which can never go far enough). 'Eternity', wrote Blake (Yeats' favourite quotation), 'is in love with the productions of Time' and I have tried to pay homage to both. But the two being interlinked, the two sets of images approach each other.[14]

The existence of this realm of the eternal, in love with the productions of time, this realm of non-being in love with, yet threatening to destroy being, is sometimes pictured in the poetry by bell images. More often it is suggested by imagery of wind and sea. It must be pointed out, however, that the 'eternity' these images suggest is remote from any normal ideas associated with that word. This is no heaven of angels, or spiritual realm where deity resides. It is no transcendent reality, more a transcendent non-reality. It is nothingness without which there would be no 'isness', it is non-being which allows for being. It is the unknown without which there could be no known. It is that which would destroy what is, and paradoxically permits it to be. The one depends on the other completely. In orthodox views of transcendence the transcendent exists irrespective of the existence of the world. For example, in orthodox Christian metaphysics God is said to exist in and for himself. In MacNeice's thought the 'eternal' is dependent on the world as the world is dependent on the 'eternal'.

In an early poem *Nocturne* (a slight but effective poem) the wind is personified as he goes

> *Slouching round the landscape.*

The poem is simply descriptive, but ends with a note of threatening, with a suggestion that it may be a wind from beyond time, from a possible eternity, that blows through the night. Nothing is explicit; it is left to the reader's imagination. The wind is imagined to

> *Sinisterly bend and dip*
> *Those hulks of cloud canvas,*
> *Probing through the elm-trees,*
> *Past the houses; and then pass*
> *To a larger emptiness.*

In *Eclogue from Iceland* it is the wind which blows to destroy the timeless moment of

> *a moment's fusion*
> *With friends or nature till the cynical wind*
> *Blew the trees pale . . .*

In *June Thunder* it is the wind which presages the destruction of the beauty of a summer's day. It destroys

> *All the flare and gusto of the unenduring*
> *Joys of a season . . .*

At one level this poem can be read as mere description. On another there is the sense of something more disturbing.

> *With an indigo sky and the garden hushed except for*
> *The treetops moving.*

> *Then the curtains in my room blow suddenly inward,*
> *The shrubbery rustles, birds fly heavily homeward,*
> *The white flowers fade to nothing on the trees and rain*
> *comes*
> *Down like a dropscene.*

There is something haunted about this hushed garden with the treetops moving. This is a wind which annuls the flowers and brings rain, putting an end to the delightful show of a summer's day. The poem may be a simple description, but one senses something more. Is this merely a natural wind, or the manifestation of some unknown but terrifying force? In other poems the wind continues to suggest more than itself, to suggest an alien, unknown reality. In *The Stygian Banks* the wind is explicitly defined as symbolic of the non-being, which in a dialectical fashion attacks and yet sustains the fecund being and becoming of the garden of reality.

> *Only an incoming wind which unlike the winds of the*
> *garden*
> . . . .
> *Flutters no paper tag on a stick in a plot,*
> *Moves no leaf; the dandelion puff balls*
> *Ignore it and we often.*

But not always for there are some

> *Who when the wind which is not like any wind known*
> *Brings to their ears from ahead the drums of the Judge-*
> *ment*
> *Slacken their pace . . .*

In *Flowers in the Interval* the poet sees himself

> *trapped on the edge of the world*
> *In the wind that troubles the galaxies . . .*

which is no natural breeze, and in imagining his experience of
love as the discovery of a sleeping princess in a castle where

> *a gay wind plays on the wheat, the plains are*
> *pearled*
> *With dew and the willows are silver in wind . . .*

he asks the astonished question

> *Can it possibly*
> *Be the same wind that harries the ends of the world?*

What has the wind round his princess's castle to do with the
wind of cosmic negation, or with the forces of non-being—the
wind which in *Autumn Sequel* 'hustles' a character

> *through that revolving door in the sky*
> *To no known point of the compass . . .*
>
> *(Canto I)*

What has this 'gay wind' to do with the whirlwind of the seventh
poem of *Visitations* where, through the curtainless window the
wind was

> *twirling the gas-drums*
> *And whipping all London away into interstellar nega-*
> *tion . . .*

or with the strange wind blowing round the petrified stasis of the
late poem *Another Cold May*?

> *The tulips tug at their roots and mourn*
> *In inaudible frequencies, the move*
> *Is the wind's, not theirs . . .*

The majority of the wind images in MacNeice's poetry present
the wind (and the force of non-being which it symbolises) as
something to be feared. It is the wind which blows the cradle
out of the tree-tops (a frequent image for death in MacNeice's
poetry)[15] and it rarely is live-giving.[16] Occasionally, however, the
attitude to the wind revealed in the imagery is ambivalent. In
Autumn Journal he asserts

> *What the wind scatters the wind saves . . .*

and in *Idle Talk* he realises that

> *The wind that makes the dead leaf fall*
> *Can also make the live leaf dance.*

Another major image of eternity, of the beyond, or non-being, in MacNeice's poetry (the sea) reveals a much greater ambivalence of attitude. A passage from 'Experiences with Images' reflects this: 'It was something alien, foreboding, dangerous, and only very rarely blue. But at the same time (since until I was ten I had only once crossed it) it was a symbol of escape.'[17]

The sea has constantly entered the literature of the European imagination, but with varying symbolic value. For MacNeice it most frequently seems to represent the eternal, that area beyond normal human experience, to which he adopts an ambivalent attitude. It is both destroyer and sustainer, to be both avoided and courted. In an early poem (*Upon this Beach—* 1932) he describes the 'drunken marble' of the sea and urges the holiday-tripper

> *Forget those waves' monstrous fatuity*
> *And boarding bus be jolly.*

Concentrate on this world and forget the great emptiness beyond, the poet advises. In *Wolves* the sea is a great force which threatens to engulf life and destroy it. In *Passage Steamer* a vision of nothingness, of the petty irrelevancy of human activity in the light of the sea's immensity, comes to the poet:

> *Back from a journey I require*
> *Some new desire, desire, desire*
> *But I find in the open sea and sun*
> *None, none, none, none;*
> *The gulls that bank around the mast*
> *Insinuate that nothing we pass is past,*
> *That all our beginnings were long since begun.*

In *Postscript to Iceland* the sea is again a destructive force, for

> *the fog-bound sirens call*
> *Ruin to the long sea-wall . . .*

and in *The Death-Wish* the sea is the nothingness, the oblivion, suicides long for,

> *mad to possess the unpossessable sea . . .*

in their impatience with the reality of living.

The sea is not always feared however. *Nostalgia* expresses a longing for 'That under-sea ding-donging' and the complex ambivalence of attitude that consideration of nothingness and the unknown evokes in the poet, is expressed in *Littoral* where we are

> *Luxuriously afraid*
> *To plump the Unknown in a bucket with a spade—*
> *Each child his own seashore.*

Carrick Revisited presents clearly the dialectic between the vastness of eternity (non-being, nothingness) and the particular, using imagery of sea and hard tangible reality in opposition.

> *Time and place—our bridgeheads into reality*
> *But also its concealment! Out of the sea*
> *We land on the Particular . . .*

In *The Strand* the sea washes away the footsteps of visitors from the sand leaving nothing behind, while in *No More Sea*

> *Dove-melting mountains, ridges gashed with water,*
> *Itinerant clouds whose rubrics never alter,*
> *Give, without oath, their testimony of silence*
> *To islanders . . .*

where the word 'silence' suggests the vast nothingness sea symbolises for MacNeice. We human beings dwell on islands in a vast empty sea of eternity, of nothingness; we 'live embroiled with ocean'. We are aware of the solidity of being, but also of the vast emptiness and silence of the sea, of non-being.

In *Mahabalipuram* the sea is a nothingness, against which the living rock of being is defiantly existent. But here the sea is also acknowledged as creator. Non-being is necessary for being in the dialectical conception of life:

> *The creator who is destroyer stands at the last point of*
> *land*
> *Featureless ...*
> *... the waves assault the temple,*
> *Living granite against dead water ...*

But the temple survives the attacks of 'squadrons of water, the dark grim chargers launched from Australia'. *Autumn Sequel* also suggests the fear of negation by sea imagery, and the existence of reality against the forces of non-reality is once again affirmed by imagery of rock against sea (as in *Mahabalipuram*):

> *this is still land, not sea,*
> *Still life not death ...*
> *... This is a room*
> *Of living people. Nothing perhaps avails*
>
> *Against the sea like rock, like doomed men against*
> *doom.*

Notes for a Biography sees the sea, once more, as a destructive force, because 'All seas are cruel, spendthrift, endless. . . .' while two other later poems are evidence of the essential ambivalence, the dialectical tension, present in the use of the sea as an image of eternal emptiness in MacNeice's poetry. *Nature Notes (The Sea)* sees it as

> *Incorrigible, ruthless,*
> *. . . .*
> *Like something or someone to whom*
> *We have to surrender, finding*
> *Through that surrender life.*

The other poem *Round the Corner* simply states (without clearly defining the attitude we should adopt towards it) that

> *Round the corner is—sooner or later—the sea.*

A book review written by MacNeice casts interesting light on the genesis of this poem, and helps our interpretation of it. In a review of Rex Warner's translation of *Poems by George Seferis*, he quotes one of that poet's poems :

We knew it that the islands were beautiful
Somewhere round about here where we are groping,
Maybe a little lower or a little higher,
No distance away at all

and MacNeice continues 'Which perhaps *is* an answer; on a plane just a shade above or below our own or just round the corner which after all is our own corner, so near and yet so far in fact, lies something which might make sense of both our past and future and so redeem our present.'[18] The sea in MacNeice's poem *Round the Corner* is to be understood as a redeeming force. The great sea of nothingness, of eternity, of the unknown can be viewed positively. This conclusion is reinforced by a note MacNeice wrote to his final volume, a few days before his death. It contains a clear reference to this poem— 'I would venture the generalisation that most of these poems are two-way affairs or at least spiral ones : even in the most evil picture the good things, like the sea in one of these poems, are still there round the corner.'[19] So for MacNeice the sea in *The Casualty* was the kingdom of death as it is in *A Hand of Snapshots, The Gone-Tomorrow* or in *Jigsaws* where 'death curls over in the wave'. But in *Western Landscape* the sea was the object of desire and longing.

Occasionally these images of bells, wind and sea are compressed into an image cluster, to form a complex new image of this aspect of MacNeice's thought. An obvious example of this is the 'under-sea ding-donging' of *Nostalgia* or the wind in *Round the Corner* which carried the smell of the sea :

a wind from round the corner
Carries the smell of wrack or the taste of salt . . .

The best example is in *Day of Renewal* where Dick Whittington hears the sound of bells :

Bronze tongues lost in a breaking wave . . .

and later in the poem

the clappers overlap in the waves
And the words are lost on the wind.

At quite the other end of the spectrum of images from these

'metaphysical' or 'mystical' examples, (of which these last are probably the most obviously mystical) are what MacNeice in 'Experiences with Images' calls 'physical' or merely 'descriptive' images. These are images which do not suggest or embody any concepts beyond themselves. They simply attempt to realise the individual, particular, given reality of a thing, to capture what Hopkins called the 'individuation' of things. Examples of such images are legion in MacNeice's poetry and it would be impossible to do other than suggest a number of examples. The opening image of *Under the Mountain* is of this type—

> *Seen from above*
> *The foam in the curving bay is a goose-quill*
> *That feathers . . . unfeathers . . . itself*

as is the image in *Littoral*,

> *The sand here looks like metal, it feels there like fur . . .*

Yet although these images out of context seem merely descriptive, in the body of MacNeice's work they are of greater significance. The dozens of images which attempt to catch the exact, particular essence of an experience, an object or a person, begin to stand for the tangible existent world itself, which in MacNeice's thought is one pole of the dialectic of life. The sea attacks the world of being, which is a world of tangible, often beautiful entities. These images give us what the poet described in *Train to Dublin* as

> *the incidental things which pass*
> *Outward through space exactly as each was.*

They evoke for us the ever-changing, existent, vigorous, fertile life of the world itself. It is the world he pictures in a passage in his prose work *Zoo* :

> The pleasure of dappled things, the beauty of adaption to purpose, the glory of extravagance, classic elegance or romantic nonsense and grotesquerie—all of these we get from the Zoo. We react to these with the same delight as to new potatoes in April speckled with chopped parsley or the light at night on the Thames of Battersea Power House, or to cars sweeping their shadows from lamp-post to lamp-post down Haverstock

Hill or to brewer's drays or to lighthouses and searchlights or to a newly-cut lawn or to a hot towel and friction at the barber's or to Moran's two classic tries at Twickenham in 1937 or to the smell of dusting-powder in a warm bathroom or to the fun of shelling peas into a china bowl or to shuffling one's feet through dead leaves when they are crisp or to the noise of rain or the crackling of a newly lit fire or the jokes of a street-hawker or the silence of snow in the moonlight or the purring of a powerful car.[20]

This is a hymn to existence itself. The same world of change, vigour and tangible reality is present in the imagery of many of the poems, flickering and flaunting its existence in the face of nothingness.

It is a world of sunlight flashing off water, of the *Mayfly* which in a magnificent line is seen to

> *Inconsequently dance above the dazzling wave* . . .[21]

or the quivering of fish in a tank as in *The Glacier* where the detailed work of the latinist is opposed to the petrification of the crawling traffic :

> *And we who have always been haunted by the fear of*
> *becoming stone*
> *Cannot bear to watch that catafalque creep down*
> *And therefore turn away to seemingly slower things*
> *And rejoice there to have found the speed of fins and*
> *wings*
> *In the minnow-twisting of the latinist who alone*
> *Nibbles and darts through the shallows of the lexicon* . . .

It is a world of 'wafers of early sunlight' and the swift fluttering movement of a viola player's hand, like a fish in a glass tank that

> *Rises, remains quivering, darts away*
> *To nibble invisible weeds.*

It is a world where

> *the sack*
> *Of night pours down on you Provençal stars* . . .

I

and a world where

> one day catches mackerel, a thousand white
>
> *Excitements flapping on a thousand hooks,*
> *And one day combs its hair with the west wind*
> *And takes its pinch and sneezes gulls and rooks . . .*

Such imagery as this in MacNeice's poetic universe becomes more than descriptive. It comes to stand for the vigorous tangible beauty of existence itself, attacked and sustained by the cold, alien, (yet ambivalently viewed) otherness and non-being of the sea.

We have explored the main landmarks of the 'geography' created by the imagery in MacNeice's poetry, demonstrating how themes we noted in the previous chapters are pictured, given poetic clothing by certain repeated images, image complexes and motifs. The sceptic's sense that the only way to find value in experience is to create it oneself, is suggested by the quest motif and its associated imagery. The progress of man, sceptical and threatened by despair, through the continually changing flux of experience which he cannot comprehend, is embodied in images of journey and travel. But his scepticism, as we insisted in Part I, is creative for it drives him to his own kind of affirmation: of life, as a fertile, dialectical tension, between being and non-being, between everything and nothing, life and death. This conception is pictured by images and image patterns of the 'eternal' and 'physical' in dialectical opposition, of a fragile world of delightful particulars threatened by negation. The poet's sceptical dislike of any absolute systems, of any transcendence, which would freeze the flux and limitedness of experience, destroying the continually processing fertility of the dialectic between life and death, is seen in his use of images of petrification and associated motifs. His images are the embodiment of creative scepticism.

5

The Image in the Poem and the Poem in the World

In critical writings on MacNeice's poetry there is a repeated complaint. The suggestion is that MacNeice is a gay conjuror with images, a poet of cunning *legerdemain* and deception. His poetry is a shallow trick, too clever by half. His skill with images is seen as a brilliant bravura decoration over an essential hollow-ness—like the decorative facades of an empty and uninhabited house. G. S. Fraser is representative when he writes of *Ten Burnt Offerings*: 'The ornamentation in fact, in this book had often the air not of emerging spontaneously from the theme, but of being trailed over it like roses over a trellis.'[1]

Yet, strangely, there is a different emphasis in MacNeice's own critical writings on the nature of poetry. He was always clearly aware that form and subject matter must be firmly wedded in poetry, that neither should be cultivated to the exclusion of the other. His early critical exercises do *in fact* emphasise communication of subject matter, somewhat neglecting formal considerations. In an early essay he wrote 'Pure poetry as we have seen it is on the decline'[2] and confessed 'In narrative, drama, propaganda, satire, etc. we shall have to compromise with the public.'[3] In 'A Statement' in *New Verse* he wrote 'the poet at the moment will tend to be moralist rather than aesthete.'[4] In an essay published in 1936 when expressing pleasure that poets were 'writing about things again'[5] he went on to remark 'Literature is made with words, and words are a means of conveying a meaning. It is no doubt possible to use words merely for decoration, as the Moors used tags of the Koran to decorate their walls at heights where no one could read them. To do this in literature seems a perversion.'[6] Throughout MacNeice's early criticism there is this vigorous attack on any mere aestheticism; there is a belief that poetry must be 'A criticism (if in a wider

sense of the word) of life'[7] and that it must *communicate* this
involved criticism. In an article in the next decade he still asserts
this: 'The critic then must start by remembering that words are
a means of communication. What is the poet trying to communicate? And does he bring it off?'[8] In his book on W. B.
Yeats, the young poet, forced to consider the older poet's origins
in ninetyish aestheticism, tried to overcome his thirties pre-
judices, to explain the older poet's success: 'Most of the poets
of the Nineties lost themselves in the sands. Yeats escaped because he harnessed the aesthetic doctrine to a force outside itself
which he found in his own country.'[9] In other words, he turned
from mere decoration to write *about* something, contemporary
concerns of Ireland.

But the emphasis in the early criticism is not entirely on the
necessity for a clearly realised, socially relevant subject matter.
It is simply that the situation as MacNeice saw it, demanded this
emphasis. MacNeice also realised that poetry must be a finely
worked out relationship between subject matter and form. He
wrote in *Modern Poetry* that 'The essence of the poetry does
not lie in the thing described or in the message imparted but
in the resulting concrete unity, the poem.'[10] Note the phrase
'concrete unity'. In his book on Yeats he wrote: 'The relationship between form and matter is like a marriage; matter must
find itself in form and form must find itself in matter.'[11] From
MacNeice's criticism it would seem that we have the prescrip-
tion for a poetry which would scorn to use an image merely for its
decorative effect, for the simple beauty of the image itself, irrespective of its context in the poem, and as a comment on the world.

Yet one can detect shades and suggestions of another point of
view in his early criticism too. He wrote at Oxford (not long
before publication of his first volume *Blind Fireworks*): 'If you
must write poetry, don't decline the charge of artificiality. It
is only a further link in the chain of artifices—Life, men, society,
language. The more the sounder.'[12] The slightly petulant air
about this suggests he is defending the artificiality, the false
decorativeness of his own early ideas. He could quite cheerfully
characterise poems in his first book, as 'artificial and yet random;
because they go quickly through their antics against an important background.'[13] In this volume the artificial fireworks somewhat obscure the important background. The imagery is self-

consciously ostentatious. The decorativeness is flaunted. So Mac-Neice wrote in *Modern Poetry*: 'Though sympathising with the present-day demand for concentration and economy in poetry, I have never conceded to the extremists that a great book is necessarily a great evil or that mere decoration is necessarily vicious.'[14]

It would seem that there were two elements in MacNeice's thinking on poetry. The mature poet was sure of what poetry ought to be—an engaged criticism of life, communicating with the public, in verse which perfectly weds subject and form; the other (the residue of his youthful enthusiasms) was tempted to regard imaginative conceits and elaborate decorativeness as worthwhile in and of themselves.

In his early poetry, despite the criticism, the second kind of poetry is often evident. There are many of the kind of images which MacNeice was later to describe as 'random decoration'.[15] A passage from 'Experiences with Images' clarifies what he meant by this: 'In *Poems* and *The Earth Compels* my images, attached to details, were usually details in themselves. They could therefore be judged by their *correspondence* to particular objects or events.'[16] Such poetry must be flawed. For an image can never be judged solely by its correspondence to a thing or an event, but must also be judged by its relation to the total context in which it appears, the poem as a whole, (which it helps to create). C. Day Lewis writes well of the double relationship of an image to the thing described, and to the poem in which it appears: 'The image is a drawing back from the actual, the better to come to grips with it: so every successful image is the sign of a successful encounter with the real. When an image fails, we may trace the defect technically—it is inconsistent, too weak or too strong for its context . . .'[17] When an image is included for its decorative effect or solely because it captures the essence of a particular thing or event (without due regard for its context) it tends to destroy the poem. It seems to be merely fanciful.

In a poem like MacNeice's early *Evening Indoors,* non-structural, decorative imagery mars the totality of the poem. The images have a certain justness of correspondence, as well as a certain beauty, but they do not fuse into an organic unity. I quote part of the poem:

> *The glass fringe of the shade seems a summer waterfall,*
> *Like August insects purring over mown grass*
> *The flames blend and pass, incend and end and pass.*
> *Like the calm blue marriage of the sky and sea,*
> *Or a blue-veiled Madonna beaming vacancy,*
> *See that Madonna snuff out the shaded light*
> *And stroke with soothing hand asleep the night.*

The image of 'the Madonna beaming vacancy' is discordant. How is this related to a 'summer waterfall'? What is the purpose of their relation? This seems a piece of free associationism, not the organic unity which is a poem.

   This predilection for imagery of a garish poster-colour brilliance and artificiality, which decorates, yet mars, MacNeice's early poetry, can be seen very clearly in the poem *Ode*. In a poem of largely philosophic discussion we are interrupted by a passage of garish colour, almost vulgar in context. It is loud, overdone (in another context of course it could be perfectly effective) :

> *The leaves dark green on top, light green under, seas of*
> *green*
> *Had brought him on full flood, the colour laid on in*
> *slices*
> *As by a mason's trowel or ice cream in sliders*
> *Bought in dusty streets under the yellow-green beeches,*
> *A little while ago the green was only peppered*
> *But now we gape at a wealthy wave and a tidal tower of*
> *green.*

The images preen themselves with narcissistic self-delight. Years later such self-indulgence crops up again with an enervating frequency in *Autumn Sequel*. Such imagery is brilliant, colourful, garish, but ultimately one distrusts it as a shallow bravura. It is related in MacNeice's work to the facile chicness, the over-clever mental agility of passages such as :

> *The young man grieves*
> *To receive the account in red—red on the tree*
> *Or on the evening sky . . .*
>
> *(Autumn Sequel, Canto II)*

It has the effect on the reader of directing him to the wit of colourfulness of the image itself. Modishly unsatisfactory, it reminds of the flashy evocation of the sea in Canto V of *Autumn Sequel*:

> *One great swish*
>
> *Of seaweed, and a cruel comber broke*
> *About the table legs in marbled scum,*
> *And polypods and squids and deep sea folk*
>
> *Burst in with longshore fife and deep-sea drum*
> *And pennons and scarves of spindrift, agog to see*
> *Their long suit proven and their kingdom come . . .*

Here each image may be an accurate correspondence, but the passage lacks unifying imaginative power at work except, possibly, the force of parody.

But frequent usage of non-structural imagery in MacNeice's early and middle verse has a much more significant effect on the reader. Images float free from poems, bright, particular, unrelated to the structures which they fracture, to suggest the independence, the nominal nature, of the sense impressions they capture. The poems' structures fragment to suggest a sceptical distrust of even those poems' own organisation. Such poems suggest the plural disorganisation of an experience which refuses to be captured completely in a poem, in a structural form:

> *We cannot cage the minute*
> *Within its nets of gold.*

So, I would argue, MacNeice's use of non-structural imagery suggests, and may be the result of, a scepticism of even the poem's ability to create order, pattern and meaning of the flux of experience. The objects and images themselves in the early poems constantly disrupt the pattern which the poem tries to make. The non-structural quality of the poet's imagery is an embodiment of his radical scepticism.

But one can tire quickly of such verse, and it tends by its very nature to be as ephemeral as the flux it imitates. It interests superficially but comes to be seen as imaginatively incoherent as well as structurally so.

It is perfectly clear that MacNeice realised the need to purge his poetry of such imagery, for in the dedication to poems written in the period 1941–44 he wrote :

> *Because the velvet image,*
> *Because the lilting measure,*
> *No more convey my meaning*
> *I am compelled to use*
> *Such words as disabuse*
> *My mind of casual pleasure*
> *And turn it towards a centre.*

In 'Experiences with Images' (1949) he indicated his closer concern with the total structure of a poem : 'All poems, as I said above, are dramatic. Since *Autumn Journal* I have been eschewing the news-reel and attempting a stricter kind of drama which largely depends upon structure.'[18] Upon analysis he feels that 'this structural tightening up'[19] seems to involve, among other things, 'a more structural use of imagery'[20] and he writes that 'when we come to the more important structural type of image the criterion of mere correspondence will often fail us.'[21] His new interest and commitment is made even clearer when he writes later in the essay 'The sort of poem I am now trying to write is meant to be all of a piece'[22] and the intention to eschew what he calls 'the romantic elaboration of glamour images'[23] is made obvious by his conclusion : 'I would end by repeating that an image is not an end in itself; only the poem is the end, that dramatic unity which must have its downs as well as its ups but which, above all, must be self-coherent. A dull image, a halting rhythm, a threadbare piece of diction, which further that end, are far, far better than a sparkling image, a delightful rhythm or a noble piece of diction which impede it.'[24]

It is interesting that MacNeice sensed the need for this in drama, long before he wrote these words about poetry. In 1938 he wrote 'If we are going to do justice to the complexity and contradictions and concealed relevances of the modern world, we must bolster up or girder our plays into as much unity as we can.'[25] This may explain why, when he came to feel the need of structural unity in a poem he expressed it in terms such as 'a stricter kind of drama which largely depends on structure.'[26]

In an introduction to the first edition of *Christopher Columbus*, published in 1944, MacNeice makes the connection between structure in a drama and in a poem: 'If radio drama is poetic, its poetry—like poetry in general—must consist of a great deal more than rhythmical patterns of words; it presupposes a wider and deeper pattern beginning with a careful and intuitive selection of material and culminating in a larger architectonic. The first value of a radio script is construction.'[27] One also notes that three years after the important article on images we find the poet praising George Herbert's command of organic structure: 'Dr. Johnson, discussing the Metaphysical poets in his life of Cowley, does not mention Herbert, and this is significant, for Johnson there is doing unkindly what we in our time may have done in mistaken adulation, picking out strained conceits which throw their poems out of balance—and he picks them out because they *stick out*. Herbert's conceits very rarely stick out offendingly but are usually organic parts of a whole; nearly all his poems are in balance. His first virtue is *construction*.'[28] Two years later he again praises Herbert for 'the organic structure of his poems'.[29]

The best way to indicate the very real change in the structural organisation of imagery, which is observable in MacNeice's poetry, concurrent with this thinking, is to compare two short poems of different periods. First an early poem *Now that the Shapes of Mist*:

> *Now that the shapes of mist like hooded beggar-children*
> *Slink quickly along the middle of the road*
> *And the lamps draw trails of milk in ponds of lustrous*
> > *lead*
> *I am decidedly pleased not to be dead.*
>
> *Or when wet roads at night reflect the clutching*
> *Importunate fingers of trees and windy shadows*
> *Lunge and flounce on the windscreen as I drive*
> *I am glad of the accident of being alive.*
>
> *There are so many nights with stars or close-*
> *ly interleaved with battleship-grey or plum,*
> *So many visitors whose Buddha-like palms are pressed*
> *Against the windowpanes where people take their rest.*

Whose favour now is yours to screen your sleep—
You need not hear the strings that are tuning for the
dawn—
Mingling, my dear, your breath with the quiet breath
Of sleep whom the old writers called the brother of
Death.

This is not a good poem, and its failure can be partly traced to its disorganised use of imagery. The images lack coherence. The poem disintegrates as a total, formal artifact. The trope of the first two lines is impressive, and one wishes it would continue, but the suggestion of 'ponds of lustrous lead' introduces a discordant note, at crude variance with the delicate image of the wraithlike slinking of the mist. The image has been included for its own sake, without due regard to what has gone before. Stanza two continues to personify the outside world of a night scene, and maintains the suggestion of the airy, phantom-like insubstantial nature of the personified entities, with the phrase 'windy shadows'. The third stanza however introduces ideas and associations which seem totally irrelevant. Indeed, it is difficult to construe. The phrase 'battleship-grey or plum' has unfortunately absurd connotations. It is utterly non-structural as is the phrase 'Buddha-like palms', the meaning of which is also obscure. What does the phrase 'Buddha-like palms' mean in the total context of this poem? It is unnecessarily obtrusive, creating irrelevant associations. The final stanza introduces another subject—a romantic apostrophe (this has not been prepared for in the rest of the poem). One wonders what relationship the new imagery of music is meant to have with that which went before. The line 'You need not hear the strings that are tuning for the dawn' is beautifully written but structurally discordant for all its personal music. One wonders also what the reference to 'the old writers' has to do with the rest, apart from its attempt to give the poem a bogus dignity and importance, which has not been worked for. The individual images of this poem are, perhaps, impressive, even exciting, but they do not fuse with one another. There is a disharmony in the poem. Its structure fragments at points. We meet here what Michael Longley has called MacNeice's 'impatience, that refusal to let his ideas settle to a depth, which in his lesser poems results in surfaces made brilliant in order to cover up imaginative inconsistencies . . .'[30] There is no imaginative coherence in depth, rather a surface of flashy, witty, but ultimately unrelated, non-structural, imagery. The second poem from a later volume that I suggest by way of comparison, is *Death of an Old Lady*:

> *At five in the morning there were grey voices*
> *Calling three times through the dank fields;*
> *The ground fell away beyond the voices*
> *Forty long years to the wrinkled lough*
> *That had given a child one shining glimpse*
> *Of a boat so big it was named Titanic.*
>
> *Named or called? For a name is a call—*
> *Shipyard voices at five in the morning,*
> *As now for this old tired lady who sails*
> *Towards her own iceberg calm and slow;*
> *We hardly hear the screws, we hardly*
> *Can think her back her four score years.*
>
> *They called and ceased. Later the night nurse*
> *Handed over, the day went down*
> *To the sea in a ship, it was grey April,*
> *The daffodils in her garden waited*
> *To make her a wreath, the iceberg waited;*
> *At eight in the evening the ship went down.*

This is powerful, mature poetry. Organised around the central trope of death as the Titanic striking the iceberg, the imagery is muted and unobtrusive. Yet each particular image contributes with a delicate and moving accuracy to the total effect. The 'grey voices' of the first line creates the required sombre atmosphere, as does the phrase 'dank fields'. The sudden falling away of the ground has a peculiar imaginative effect; it suggests death itself, while 'wrinkled lough' reminds one almost unconsciously of the poem's subject, the old lady, and the phrase 'shining glimpse' stands out effectively amongst the grey muted imagery of the stanza. This latter phrase as a kind of indirect reference to the old lady, who is a ship sailing towards her own iceberg, endows her with a certain nobility and beauty, proper to her. The suggestion in the shipyard voices, of the world of men and work, of activity, which she is leaving, is most moving in stanza two, while in stanza three the Biblical echo in the imagery contributes accurately to the sombre celebration, the dignified evocation of the old lady's death. The fact that the daffodils are waiting as well as the iceberg, is haunting, for it gives to the April daffodils, which will make the wreath, a disturbing coldness as of ice, while to the iceberg itself is imparted something of the fragile beauty of the daffodils. This poignant ambiguity is then resolved by the final image of the ship sinking, the old lady dies. The whole poem is of a piece; it is a coherent organic whole; the images fuse together and none seems merely there for its own beauty or wit, merely for its decorative effect.

This latter poem derives most of its structurally tight organisation from the fact that it is organised round a central trope, round what MacNeice in 'Experiences with Images' called 'the *rational* metaphor'.[31] Around this all the other images cluster. MacNeice cites the poem *Convoy* as an example of this with its simple statement that life is like a steady, determined convoy dependent 'upon pragmatic/And ruthless attitudes—destroyers and corvettes'. Yet in *Death of an Old Lady* we are aware of other organising forces at work, especially in the image 'The ground fell away beyond the voices/Forty long years ago' with its peculiar suggestions of death. Some strange logic of the imagination is in operation. MacNeice sometimes organises his poems by the strange principles of imaginative logic. This strange logic he associates with dreams in 'Experiences with Images', writing that '*The Springboard*, though rational in its working out, begins with two irrational premises—the dream picture of a naked man standing on a springboard in the middle of the air over London and the irrational assumption that it is his duty to throw himself down from there as a sort of ritual sacrifice. This will be lost on those who have no dream logic . . .'[32] When we surrender to the imaginative picture it is a strangely powerful poem with images of Christian sacrifice clashing disturbingly with the doubting of the central character. It is a structural whole bound together by this dream logic. It is when we imaginatively surrender to the nightmare conditions of a poem such as *Hold-Up*, when everything freezes as in a dream, that we see the subtle structural accuracy of describing a man in a telephone kiosk in the following lurid terms :

> *a tall glass box*
> *On the pavement held a corpse in pickle*
> *His ear still cocked . . .*

In another context this would be in bad taste, or absurd or amusing; here it contributes horrifyingly to the total structure of the poem, in fact helping to create it. It will not, however, fulfil its function unless we surrender imaginatively to the poem.

MacNeice occasionally uses another organising principle in his poetry which in his essay on images he describes in the following terms; he states that in 'some poems . . . I have used a set of basic images which crossfade into each other'.[33] Having cited by way of example *Homage to Clichés,* he continues : 'The same quasi-musical interlinking of images, with variations on contrasted themes, is used in a recent short poem of mine *Slow Movement,* and with a more leisurely accumulative effect, in a recent long poem, *The Stygian Banks*'.[34] In *Slow Movement* we find it at work to good effect, as the images phase into each other like the themes and connected counter themes of a piece of music, to reach the climax of the fifth stanza which organises its images in as nearly a contrapuntal fashion as language will allow. The train, music and aquarium images which have been present in earlier stanzas are all included in the poem's penultimate lines :

> *The movement ends, the train has come to a stop*
> *In buttercup fields, the fiddles are silent, the whole*
> *Shoal of silver tessellates the aquarium*
> *Floor, not a bubble rises . . .*

The technique is successful as a mode of structural organisation; the poem is of a piece. In the longer *Stygian Banks* one notes the same repetition of image complexes as if they were musical themes in a symphony, but the technique does not have the same success there. In the extended, discursive and, it must be admitted, occasionally tedious blank verse, such a method of organisation seems arbitrarily applied from the outside, rather than, as it appears in the shorter poem, a manifestation of some internal principle of the poem itself. Yet when this technique succeeds it is most effective, as in *Slow Movement* or as in the perhaps less tightly organised poem *Homage to Clichés.*

So in MacNeice's poetry can be seen a development in the poet's use of imagery. From an early ability to coin bright flashy images, sometimes without due regard to the context in which they appeared, the poet came to use images structurally, giving attention to their relation to their whole environment. We see that he attempted to achieve this in three ways—by building a poem round a central rational trope, by attempting to follow musical techniques in phasing and cross-phasing similar and contrasted images into each other, and by trying to organise the images of a poem with regard to the logic of the imagination, the strange yet unifying logic of dreams.

MacNeice was keenly interested in dreams and dreamlore, in their causes and significance. In *The Strings are False* he describes at length a number of his own nightmares and dreams. Now it seems to me that the description of a dream in a work of literature naturally inclines the reader to look for hidden meaning in the work. It is then a short step from seeing a dream in literature as significant, to seeing it as allegory. For allegory is the presentation in material picturable terms, within an imaginatively created world, of abstract concepts. When Pilgrim in Bunyan's allegory meets the horrifying figure of Apollyon, we see in their battle not merely an exciting conflict, but the eternal conflict of the Christian soul with the forces of evil. We see in picture-terms a vicious struggle, which has a meaning beyond itself in its representation of an intellectual or spiritual struggle.

Allegory is literature which creates a self-consistent world (in which events take place) whose main purpose is to have a special relationship with the real world. It does not primarily exist for itself but for its significance, as an embodiment of ideas, or abstractions or spiritual realities. Edwin Honig in his book on allegory *Dark Conceit* expresses it thus : 'The double purpose of *making* a reality and making it *mean* something is peculiar to allegory and its directive language.'[35] This gives us a vital clue to the nature of allegory as distinct from other literature. Allegory is the creation within a literary structure of a special world, in order to represent or suggest some qualities in the real world. One has of course an uneasy sense that this definition applies to all literature, that all literature is, to a degree, allegorical. Even a distinctly 'realist' poem such as Browning's *Up at the Villa, Down in the City* can be read as presenting an opposition between the concepts of town life and country life, and in that sense could be described as an allegory. Yet here it is a question of degree. Northrop Frye writes well of this : 'Within the boundaries of literature we find a kind of sliding scale, ranging from the most explicitly allegorical, consistent with being literature at all, at one extreme, to the most elusive, anti-explicit and anti-allegorical at the other.'[36] And whether we as critics view a work as allegorical or not depends on where on this sliding scale the work in question demands to be placed. Graham Hough writes, expanding Frye's insights, 'At one extreme then, the simplest kind of allegory in which the interest of the objects and the events is entirely subordinate to that of the concepts; at the other, realism, in which the interest of the concepts is entirely subordinate to that of the objects and events.'[37]

MacNeice himself has written perceptively on this problem in *Varieties of Parable* : 'In answer to the question "Can you think of any literary work that is not in some sense a parable?" one has to recognise that nearly all "realistic" fiction must be so, in however slight a sense.'[38] He suggests that the words of a literary artifact 'will stand for something not themselves; in other words, they will be symbols. So the difference between "realistic writing" and "parable writing" appears to be one of degree.'[39]

In MacNeice's work there is a considerable number of poems which demand to be placed well up on the scale towards allegory, where the objects are subordinate to the concepts, however vague these concepts may be. This demand is created by MacNeice's descriptions of dream experience and by a technique reminiscent of emblematic iconography.

It is inevitable that a reader, confronted by a poem which seems to work by dream logic, or which explicitly presents a dream world or an obviously imaginative incident, should feel that the poem is moving towards allegory, that it is in Mac-Neice's terms a 'special world'[40] with a relationship to the 'ordinary world', that it may be meant to embody intellectual concepts in picturable form. Why tell us of a dream if you do not believe it has some significance? MacNeice was always interested in the double-levelled kind of writing, of which allegory is a highly developed form. Even in the thirties when he was associated with the Auden, Spender, Day Lewis group, we hear him disclaiming constantly mere 'realism', the 'realism' of the propaganda poets. In his early essay 'Poetry' he writes 'The best poems are written on two or more planes at once, just as they are written from a multitude of motives. Poetry is essentially ambiguous, but ambiguity is not necessarily obscure.'[41] In his study of W. B. Yeats we find another early disclaimer of mere descriptive realism, in preference for a more complex (perhaps double-or-multiple-layer) kind of writing. In a passage which discusses his attitude to Eliot, Yeats, and realism he writes : 'A few years later I felt differently towards him, perhaps because I had realised that Eliot's poetry itself is largely both mannerism and fantasy and that the daylight of "realism" is itself largely a fiction.'[42] Later in the book he attacks *simpliste* views of poetry : 'The propaganda poets claim to be realists— a claim which can only be correct if realism is identical with pragmatism. Truth, whether poetic or scientific, tends as often as not to be neither simple nor easily intelligible. . . .'[43] This outlook, that art may be something quite different from description, from strict mimesis, becomes even more explicit in his introduction to a group of radio plays, especially in the introduction to *The Dark Tower*. Here MacNeice wrote :

The Dark Tower is a parable play, belonging to that wide class of writings which includes *Everyman*, *The Faerie Queen* and *The Pilgrim's Progress*. Though under the name of allegory this kind of writing is sometimes dismissed as outmoded, the clothed as distinct from the naked allegory is in fact very much alive . . . My own impression is that pure 'realism' is in our time almost played out, though most works of fiction will remain realistic *on the surface*. The single track mind and the single-plane novel or play are almost bound to falsify the world in which we live. The fact that there is method in madness and the fact that there is fact in fantasy (and equally fantasy in 'fact') have been brought home to us not only by Freud and other psychologists but by events themselves. This being so, reportage can no longer masquerade as art. So the novelist, abandoning the 'straight' method of photography, is likely to resort once more not only to the twist of plot but to all kinds of other twists which may help him to do justice to the world's complexity. Some element of parable therefore, far from making a work thinner and more abstract, ought to make it more concrete. Man does after all live by symbols.[44]

Note here the association (suggested by reference to Freud) of such literature with dreams and fantasy.

In later writings this interest in parable or allegory writing becomes even more explicit; it is almost always associated with dreams and fantasies, as in the passage above. Even in an essay where MacNeice is dealing with the importance of a poet's communication with his public, he is at pains to point out that 'Every poet knows that poetic sense is not the same as common sense.'[45] It may use the logic of the imagination or of dream. In 'Experiences with Images' he writes (as we noted) that ' "Springboard" will be lost on those who have no dream logic, as will other poems of mine such as "The Dowser" and "Order to View" *which are a blend of rational allegory and dream suggestiveness.'*[46] (My italics.)

It is of course in MacNeice's series of lectures called *Varieties of Parable* that this interest in allegory and dream is most developed. This work is a broad survey of allegory writing in English. A brilliantly sensitive book, perhaps its most interesting aspect is the light it throws on the poet's own poetic practice. Once again in this work we find the association of allegory and parable with dream :

This dubious ground which I am exploring attracted me in three of my capacities, as a person, as a poet and as a practitioner in sound radio. As a person I have from childhood been a steady dreamer (I mean in the literal sense) and I have never been tempted to dismiss dreams as 'insubstantial' or 'unreal'; long before I read the psychologists, I took it for granted that my dreams had a lot to do with me my self and my world . . .

In poetry, as a reader I have fairly catholic tastes but I would rather read Spenser than most; this is because of his exceptional depth and variety and because his work has the richness and complexity of the best dreams and the truth to life of the best fairy stories.[47]

Dreams and allegory seem to be very closely linked in Mac-Neice's thinking.

K

Throughout his poetry there are poems, suggestive of dreams, which strain towards the condition of allegory. An artifact has been created to mean, as well as to describe.

The dream quality of such poetry prompts consideration of significance. We seek for an abstract concept or spiritual reality of which the poem is a pictorial embodiment. The first stanza of *Order to View* will give some indication of this :

> *It was a big house, bleak;*
> *Grass on the drive;*
> *We had been there before*
> *But memory, weak in front of*
> *A blistered door, could find*
> *Nothing alive now;*
> *The shrubbery dripped, a crypt*
> *Of leafmould dreams; a tarnished*
> *Arrow over an empty stable*
> *Shifted a little in the tenuous wind,*
>
> *And wishes were unable*
> *To rise . . .*

This creates, with its flat bare statement, a peculiar, unreal atmosphere. There is a strange fusion between subjective and objective experience as in trance or delirium. The crypt is a crypt of leafmould dreams, while wishes cannot rise in the almost windless air. It is a special landscape assembled from constituents of the normal world. It tempts us to ask, what does it mean? Another poem of this semi-allegorical nature (what MacNeice calls 'a blend of rational allegory and dream suggestiveness'[48]) is *The Rest House*. It opens again in a strange dreamlike landscape. 'The thick night fell, the folding table unfolded . . .' The scene is alive, objects have an unpleasant spontaneous life of their own. The description which follows :

> *The hissing lamp had hypnotised the lizards*
> *That splayed their baby hands on the wired window . . .*

is particularly suggestive of nightmare experience. This seems to be no natural landscape, but an inner imaginative world. The second stanza strangely suggests birth and death :

> *The bed beneath the ghostly netting beckoned*
> *To chrysalid or sepulchral sleep.*

Reading the final lines:

> *But such*
> *Was now the river's dominance that he filtered*
> *Through even the deepest sleep, weaving his journey*
> *Out of too little history into too much . . .*

we wonder if this is some allegorical river of life, winding from birth to death. The suggestion is implicit.

In MacNeice's later poems, such interior mental landscapes, dream experiences, become more frequent (perhaps as his interest in parable became greater). This forces one to ask of their meaning.[49] Certainly they are special worlds and seem created to mean something. Yet disturbingly one cannot quite put a meaning to them. They are strangely suggestive, but not explicit. They seem to say 'He that hath ears to hear let him hear.' One of the best of these is *After the Crash*. The first stanza moves with the assured illogic of a dream. It has its own kind of illogical logic.

> *When he came to he knew*
> *Time must have passed because*
> *The asphalt was high with hemlock . . .*

The 'because' here is quite illogical. The asphalt high with hemlock does not necessarily mean time has passed. It means rather that the cyclist is in the realm of nightmare. But in the dreamworld we accept such logic without quibble. The last stanza suggests an allegorical vision of judgment, but its meaning remains finally inexplicable:

> *Then he looked up and marked*
> *The gigantic scales in the sky,*
> *The pan on the left dead empty*
> *And the pan on the right dead empty,*
> *And he knew in the dead, dead calm*
> *It was too late to die.*

Now it may in fact be strictly inaccurate to describe such poems as allegory, if we mean by the term a strict one-to-one correspondence between image and concept. Obviously this is not allegory of that kind. Here we have the image, and sense that it is made to relate to some concept, but what that concept is, remains ultimately mysterious. Poems such as these seem to be straining towards an allegorical representation of something we are not rationally aware of. The conceptual meaning is left opaque. We just don't know how to interpret them. In *Varieties of Parable* MacNeice quotes with approval from Edwin Honig's book *Dark Conceit*, and the quotation helps to explain the peculiar puzzle-like quality of much modern allegory, including MacNeice's own : 'Some explanation for the elusive pattern and the increasing ambiguity in modern allegories may be found in the destruction of the rigid base of cultural authority upon which allegory traditionally depended and in the relatively greater stress put upon the autonomy of the artist since the Reformation.'[50]

This casts light on MacNeice's obvious defects in some allegorical poems. The longest of these is Cantos XIV–XVI of *Autumn Sequel*. The poem begins by imagining young men setting out on a quest :

> *Young men with dead leaves plastered on their shoes*
> *Set out with scrip or briefcase through the dark*
> . . . .
> *This very night they may cross the Bridge of Booze*
>
> *Into the Castle Crapulous . . .*

The names suggest the allegorical worlds of Spenser or of Bunyan as the phrase 'leaning on The Staff of Conscience' reminds of the allegorical poem attributed to Sir Walter Raleigh, *The Passionate Man's Pilgrimage*. Some of the young men enter a *Palace of Art,* and one youth dives through the canvas of one of the pictures :

> *The unsound*
>
> *Canvas collapses and he tumbles through*
> *Into a silence that vibrates . . .*

An extraordinary vision follows, a hotch-potch of allegorical motifs and personages. The hero begins climbing a spiral stair, like a soul in Dante's purgatory; then he enters a black labyrinth, where he encounters a host of workers, clad in overalls, who gather to greet their queen, who might be the Queen of Hearts from *Alice in Wonderland* :

> *Now the guards*
> *Of honour clack their mandibles, divide*
>
> *Into two ranks and, starched as playing cards,*
> *Await what comes—and what comes is their queen*
> *Surrounded by her court of drones and bards . . .*

The strange queen rises into the air followed by the wondering gaze of the masses. In the air she meets and makes love with 'the poor cause' who 'has won his frail wings too/And already is gaining air'. At the end of this part of the vision is the hint that what we have been witnessing is a marriage of the abstract qualities of love and freedom : 'every thing has been said/Of love and freedom'. But the vision changes swiftly, with the surrealistic suddenness of a dream, and the young man is whisked away by a fairground barker on a horrifying joyride, through another labyrinth, this time like the inwards of a living creature, where he hears a voice :

> *I do no work for ever; in the van*
> *Of nature I am I, who live both in*
> *And on man's guts and so have conquered man.*
>
> *Progress, my friend! Would you rather call it original*
> *sin?*

In the next canto this vision forces the young man to doubt the value of living; wandering through the guts of life he is almost about to agree : 'If life means rising skywards but to fall,/Who would choose life?' Happily he defies the temptation to deny, the vision melts away and 'The young man spirals back into his day/Where it is still the Fall'. This clearly is an allegory, yet to my mind an unsuccessful one. Here we see the difficulty of writing allegory in the midst of cultural pluralism, without any 'base of cultural authority upon which allegory traditionally depended'.[51] We sense throughout that the events are representative of mental concepts, of an abstract message. The rising queen, and the labyrinthine, animal exterior must stand for abstractions, but we find it difficult to explain what they are.

The poet has therefore to include in the work hints as to its meaning, such as the line where 'progress' is suggested. But the relationship between image and suggested concept does not seem at all convincing. Bunyan's images in *Pilgrim's Progress* seem perfectly suited to the concepts they embody, for the images receive their significance from the cultural authority upon which they depend—Puritan religion. They do not need their meanings explained. An allegory whose images need to be specifically related to concepts seems clumsy and inept by comparison. The images will almost certainly seem arbitrary and fancifully contrived.

Yet even in our pluralistic Western European culture MacNeice can write highly convincing allegories, especially when he wishes to portray the discovery of love. The best example of these is *The Burnt Bridge* (a less successful poem of the same nature is *Good Dream*). Here the hero in a dream landscape (suggestive of allegory) journeys to find a 'shining lady' (surely suggested by the Shining Ones of *Pilgrim's Progress*). The first two stanzas give an indication of the nature of the poem :

> *So, passing through the rustic gate,*
> *He slammed it to (it broke in two)*
> *As he took quick strides to tempt his fate*
> *And the world ahead was daylight.*

> *But when he reached the haunted coombe,*
> *Glancing left, glancing right,*
> *On either ridge he glimpsed his doom*
> *And the world ahead was darkness.*

Note the suggestion of dream logic here. In line two we encounter a typical ingredient of dream, where images well up into consciousness, drawn by the sound relations of words, following their own peculiar logic. The sound of 'to' summons up the rest of the line 'it broke in two'. Now it would be foolish to demand that each image in the poem should have a directly related concept. Clearly much of the detail is to suggest the strange mysterious landscape where the feared dragon dwells in the creaking haunted wood. It awakes a strange, atmospheric world which we recognise as an allegorical representation of aspects of our own. When the hero meets his shining lady and they walk hand in hand by the side

> *Of the sea that leads to nowhere ...*

we know that this represents the discovery of love in the dark dangerous wood of our own lives. This is a moving and convincing poem, which manages to create a special world allegorically representative of an essential truth about our own. In view of the difficulty of writing successful allegory in a pluralistic society, this is a considerable achievement.

MacNeice in his late poetry also demonstrated his ability to write convincing short semi-allegorical poems, when he organised them round a central motif or ikon. These have the trenchancy and effectiveness of some of Herbert's or Henryson's short allegories. The effect of these poems is related to the fact that he uses traditional imagery and iconography deeply engrained in our culture. The poems communicate without explanation. *The Tree of Guilt* is an allegorical representation of the fact that one has to pay for one's weaknesses. At times of self-indulgence the tree of guilt (obviously suggestive of the tree in Eden which wrought our fall) seems lush and green, utterly without danger; but time passes for the hero:

> *Till he finds later, waking cold*
> *The leaves fallen, himself old,*
> *And his carved heart, though vastly grown,*
> *Not recognisably his own.*

Another poem which is very similar in technique is *The Habits*. This uses the motif of the ages of man. In each stanza enervating habits enter like allegorical personifications of the vices of a medieval morality play; they tempt and destroy the hero:

> *When they put him in rompers the habits*
> *Fanned out to close in, they were dressed*
> *In primary colours and each of them*
> *Carried a rattle and a hypodermic ...*

Each stanza is a pictorial dramatic representation of a temptation appropriate to a particular time of life—games, bonhomie, woman, and alcohol—until in the last stanza 'Everyman' (for this is what the simple 'he' suggests) is left with nothing but death. The poem is extraordinarily effective, with its dark, sombre tone and trenchant honesty. A traditional allegory in technique, it shows the genre to be a living form in modern verse. MacNeice, when he died, was perfecting this kind of poem, and from a passage in *Varieties of Parable* we know that this was the realm he wished to continue to explore.

> What I myself would now like to write, if I could, would be double-level poetry, of the type of Wordsworth's 'Resolution and Independence', and, secondly, more overt parable poems in a line of descent both from folk ballads such as 'True Thomas' and some of George Herbert's allegories in miniature such as 'Redemption'.[52]

Sadly, we were robbed of these further experiments in the writings of allegory and near allegory, by MacNeice's sudden death.

Now it is most important for my argument in this book that the poet's development towards the writing of a more structurally organised kind of poetry should not be seen as a movement away from the fundamental scepticism that his earlier, more fragmented poetry suggested. So the strategies that MacNeice adopted to enable him to organise his poems must be examined further, for they seem, to this reader at least, to be strategies of the sceptic who is also an artist. As artist he senses the need for structure in poetry, but as sceptic he fears that the organised structure of a poem may misrepresent an experienced reality of nominalist detail. The poet senses the need for good poetry to be structurally organised but fears that an organised structure may misrepresent. He cannot in all honesty simply organise the descriptive nominalist details into a poem. A structurally organised poem, to the sceptic, must have a less simple relationship to reality than strict one-for-one mimesis. Thus he is driven to certain strategies, among which are double-level writing, 'overt and covert parables.'[53]

For the parable is an oblique manner of confronting the world, and of suggesting or implying meaning in it. All good parables must be prefixed with the words 'He that hath ears to hear let him hear'. Thus the teller of parables seems somewhat suspicious or sceptical of the normal modes of commenting on and ordering reality. He attacks in an oblique, ambiguous manner, in parables which may mean much, or nothing. In

MacNeice's terms: 'The single-track mind and the single-plane novel or play are almost bound to falsify the world in which we live.'[54] The parable-writer distrusts an organised, structured realism, but creates the unified world of his 'dark conceit', leaving his hearers to discern whether it has any meaningful relationship to life or not. He warns us 'do not ask me what Ism it illustrates or what Solution it offers. You do not normally ask for such things in single-plane work; why should they be forced upon something much more complex?'[55]

Such organised structures as parables, may be capable of many interpretations. Modern parables especially, as I have pointed out, have a taunting ambiguity. One cannot be exactly sure what they mean, what is their relationship with reality and with life. MacNeice in *Varieties of Parable* speaks of the multiplicity of interpretations which a parable can admit. He is discussing the work of a modern critic:

> Thus Esslin writes of *The Birthday Party* that it 'has been interpreted as an allegory of the pressures of conformity. . . . Yet the play can equally well be seen as an allegory of death'. This constitutional ambiguity—or double-level writing—is something that is often found today among poets. But those readers who have had too much of it and would write it off as a typical modern disease should remember that Spenser often practised something of the sort.[56]

In a further vital passage MacNeice quotes a critic of Kafka's work, and comments on his remarks:

> Mr Gray suggests that other critics may have gone astray because they treat Kafka as though he were 'a priest or psychologist who mistook his vocation', whereas Mr Gray— rightly, I think—prefers to treat him 'as a literary artist, not inventing complex equivalents for a system of beliefs already held, but exploring the possibilities of an image which presented itself to his imagination, in this case the image of a castle and of a man trying to reach it.' Now this, as we have seen, seems to have been the procedure—at least at moments —even of a professedly allegorical writer like Spenser. And this is often the procedure when one writes a poem. Which brings me back to the point of 'irreducibility'. Whatever the

basic beliefs implicit in *The Castle*, the book cannot be reduced to a mere exposition of such beliefs. If you expound something, that something is not only prior to but more important than the work in which you embody it.[57]

The meaning of parable, the structuring and ordering of the work is implicit within the work itself, not imposed upon it from beyond itself. The meaning is not imposed on it from without, by a necessarily ordered, meaningful reality. The writer of a parable explores an image (therefore enabling the work to be structurally organised, a self-consistent special world) which may or may not have a relationship of meaning with the real world. The writer is forced to this position because of his scepticism or distrust of simpler ways of commenting on a complex reality. As MacNeice concludes, 'All good parable writers are concerned with truth and it often is the kind of truth that cannot be, or can hardly be, expressed in other ways.'[58] But because the parable is finally irreducible, the poet takes the risk that it may not have any meaning at all, apart from its own self-consistency. A poem like *After the Crash* suggests much, may mean much. It may, however, mean nothing at all. The poet, in exploring the image his imagination has presented to him, runs the risk that he will create a special world which has no relationship of meaning to the real world. Only a radical scepticism of other methods of examining experience and reality, together with a desire to be more than a verbal photographer of fragmentary sense impressions in disorganised poems, would lead the poet to take such a risk. Yet we are often grateful when a writer does so. As John Holloway writes in a fascinating article on the poetry of Edwin Muir (another modern allegorist) 'Light cast from a great distance may carry its own decisive revelation.'[59] He remarks of one of Muir's parables

it seems—as if the poet has broken through . . . as if through a surface, and has confronted us, by what is a kind of skeletal presentation, with the essential quality of a deeply disturbing reality. Not, if you like, the suave intricacies of day-time observations, but the poignant or frightening diagrams of dream or nightmare . . . which rivet the attention and at their most powerful seem to stamp themselves indelibly on the mind.[60]

They do this not only because of their own intrinsic fascination as special worlds, but because they seem to say something true about our world. Holloway writes of Muir's poem *Milton*, 'To wander in this imaginary landscape, to experience its strangeness and terror, is to re-enter our own landscape by an unexpected and revelatory gate.'[61] Such a re-entry occurs in *After the Crash* where we feel that the nightmare world tells us something of our real world. We live after a crash, after some cosmic catastrophe, which has rendered the world a place where

hens

Fire themselves black in the batteries
And the silence of small blind cats
Debating whether to pounce . . .

can be heard. Overheard are the gigantic scales of judgment, ominous in the dead calm. We live after the fall, and for this we are to be judged and found wanting. But one must not over-interpret. The poem may be an allegory of original sin and judgment, or it may not be. The image is explored by the sceptical poet in the hope that it will by an indirect means reveal some truth which no simpler approach could discover. The poem in its ambiguity seeks to resist all rational explanation.

Thus as MacNeice developed towards a concern to write poems in which images are used structurally he concurrently developed towards the writing of parable which permitted him to write structural poems without suggesting that the pattern and order so created within the poem, were a reflection of a prior order in reality. They may be, or they may not. The poem is creating a special world, not directly describing the real one. MacNeice's interest in parables, the oblique, ambiguous raid on reality, is an indication of his basic scepticism, as his parables are an embodiment of it.

As we also noted MacNeice sometimes used a 'quasi-musical interlinking of images, with variations on contrasted themes' as a method of giving his poems unified structure. This also allowed the sceptic to write organised poems, without suggesting that the organisation is explicit in the world from which he selects details to use as images in his poem.[62] The images in these poems fade into each other as do the sounds in music. These poems again (such as in *Homage to Clichés* and *Slow Movement*) are special worlds, as a piece of music is a special world of sounds. The images are part of, and help create, a pattern, only within the structure of the poem, as sounds in music are only meaningful within the formal structure of the work itself. Music (apart from programme music) is a special world which does not refer to anything beyond itself. The sounds *mean* in relation to each other. In attempting to organise poems which approach the condition of music, MacNeice further betrays his scepticism of poetry being able to comment directly on reality in structural forms. Directly commenting on, or describing reality in organised structures may falsify it by suggesting a correspondence between the formal unity of the poem and the things described. It may imply the same formal unified structure in reality. Therefore the only expedient is to create a special world (such as parable, or a poem approaching the condition of music, or a poem obviously organised around a central literary trope or ikon, the 'rational metaphor' which reveals the poem's existence as artifice) which will not be taken for a *realistic* description, and which may or may not have a relationship to reality. So sceptic and artist can both be satisfied.

6

Scepticism: Its Language and its Forms

MacNeice is a technical virtuoso. He is a professional poet. The variety of poetic forms that he employed, frequently with an assured mastery, is amazing. He is the poet of leisurely, rambling, loose verse, and of taut, elliptical, gnomic utterance. He wrote ballads and nursery-rhyme and light, sparkling verse. He was also capable of maintaining the difficult *terza rima* verse form through the twenty-four cantos of *Autumn Sequel,* which, although it is a very uneven work, has passages of great beauty.[1] Faced with such fecundity the critic can only point to particular examples of the poet's writing in a certain form, as representative of the total work in that form. In the ballad we have such rollicking pieces as *The Streets of Laredo* (which uses the rhythms and stanza of a cowboy song) and *Bagpipe Music.* In these, the verse form and the context work together to produce a scarifying violence, a fantasia of almost surrealistic effects :

> *O early one morning I walked out like Agag,*
> *Early one morning to walk through the fire*
> *Dodging the pythons that leaked on the pavements*
> *With tinkle of glasses and tangle of wire . . .*

> *John MacDonald found a corpse, put it under the sofa,*
> *Waited till it came to life and hit it with a poker,*
> *Sold its eyes for souvenirs, sold its blood for whiskey,*
> *Kept its bones for dumb-bells to use when he was fifty.*

This is to use the traditional ballad form to brilliant effect. These two poems (and a number of others) suggest the horrifying violence which is so close to the surface of modern life, where cities can be laid waste and the crime of violence is a common-place.

The Streets of Laredo is fierce with moral indignation at wreckage and destruction. The note of indignation is created partly by the ironic discord between the subject matter and the rollicking rhythms, but also by description of the two prophet-like, denunciatory figures of Bunyan and Blake:

> *Then twangling their bibles with wrath in their nostrils*
> *From Bonehill Fields came Bunyan and Blake:*
> *'Laredo the golden is fallen, is fallen;*
> *Your flame shall not quench nor your thirst shall not*
> *slake.'*

Bagpipe Music has a nihilistic cruelty in its pointless violence, while both poems move from event to event with electrifying speed. The poems rush to their conclusions with a rapidity suggestive of the violence of the world, to which they record their horrified reactions.

MacNeice also makes frequent use of light verse forms, sometimes with ironic purpose but, at other times, simply for the fun of the thing. A poem like *Bar-Room Matins* employs light nursery-rhyme technique, at ironic cross purposes with the sombre subject matter. This produces potent satire. The dark subject is treated with a zestful yet disturbing tang, which the playful verse form helps to create:

> *Pretzels crackers chips and beer:*
> *Death is something that we fear*
> *But it titillates the ear.*
>
> *Anchovy almond ice and gin:*
> *All shall die though none can win;*
> *Let the Untergang begin—*
>
> *Die the soldiers, die the Jews,*
> *And all the breadless homeless queues.*
> *Give us this day our daily news.*

Other poems written in this form simply seem to relish the playfulness of language and rhythms in the sheer surface wit of a sophisticated nursery rhyme. A pleasing example of this is *April Fool* beginning:

Here come I, old April Fool,
Between March hare and nuts in May.
Fool me forward, fool me back,
Hares will dance and nuts will crack.

Here come I, my fingers crossed
Between the shuffle and the deal.
Fool me flush or fool me straight,
Queens are wild and queens will wait.

At other times MacNeice displays his ability to write witty light *vers de société*. Such a piece is *Letter to Graham and Anna*, which, if we relax and simply enjoy the thing for its own sake, is a refreshing excursion into light verse. Although it lacks somewhat the humour and subtlety of insight of Auden's *Letter to Lord Byron*, it displays MacNeice's ability to pen entertaining, epistolary, light verse: I particularly like the closing section:

Here we can practise forgetfulness without
A sense of guilt, fear of the tout and lout,
And here—but Wystan has butted in again
To say we must go out in the frightful rain
To see a man about a horse and so
I shall have to stop.

Elsewhere MacNeice can be deadly serious while maintaining the manner of sophisticated light verse. A heavy-handed moralistic critic might view this as irresponsibility, as a basic lack of high seriousness in the poet. But this is grossly to misread the poetry, for sometimes in the midst of apparent levity a stanza or a phrase will assess trenchantly matters of serious import. A brief phrase will encompass a vast area of experience, suggesting that the poet knows of evil and wrong, has taken it into consideration. The light verse is not irresponsible, but the almost strained reaction of a complex personality. Such poems seem to say—'I know about the evil of the world, but writing portentous, inflated moralistic poems about it won't really help.' We see this kind of deadly serious light verse[2] in *Postscript to Iceland*:

> *Not for me romantic nor*
> *Idyll on a mythic shore*
> *But a fancy turn, you know,*
> *Sandwiched in a graver show.*

> *Down in Europe Seville fell,*
> *Nations germinating hell,*
> *The Olympic Games were run—*
> *Spots upon the Aryan sun.*

That second stanza sums up the tragic, inevitable rise of Fascism in the thirties, in a few simple phrases. This is 'light' verse used to fine effect, as it is on a more personal level at the end of the same poem where the poet captures the mood of many persons of liberal sympathies, in the tense years before the war against Germany:

> *Our prerogatives as men*
> *Will be cancelled who knows when;*
> *Still I drink your health before*
> *The gun-butt raps upon the door.*

In other poems MacNeice reveals his skill in free-ranging, leisurely, discursive verse, such as the descriptive, meditative poem *The Hebrides*. It moves at a rambling, easy pace, building up a complete picture of the slow life of those islands where:

> *The west wind drops its message of indolence,*
> *No one hurries . . .*

This kind of free-ranging discursiveness is particularly effective in the long poem *Autumn Journal*, where politics, poetry, philosophy, the classics, English education, and personal experience are mingled in a loose episodic journal, written in refreshing, entertaining rhymed verse. At moments the verse form can sustain a beautiful lyricism as in the following passage from Canto IV:

> *So I give her this month and the next*
> *Though the whole of my year should be hers who has*
> *rendered already*
> *So many of its days intolerable or perplexed*
> *But so many more so happy;*

Who has left a scent on my life and left my walls
Dancing over and over with her shadow,
Whose hair is twined in all my waterfalls
And all of London littered with remembered kisses.

It can adapt itself to a conversational ease as in:

It is so hard to imagine
A world where the many would have their chance
without
A fall in the standard of intellectual living
And nothing left that the highbrow cared about . . .

(*Canto III*)

or it can tighten into a fierce, satirical brutality as in the section on the North of Ireland. Here the poet shortens the line, so that it has an urgent, bitter note, and provides blunt end-stopped sense units:

A culture built upon profit;
Free speech nipped in the bud,
The minority always guilty.
Why should I want to go back
To you, Ireland, my Ireland?

(*Canto XVI*)

In this work, the rambling, adaptable verse form is perfectly suited to suggest the characteristics of a journal (spontaneity, immediacy, a blend of public and private concerns) recording the day-to-day experiences and thoughts of an intelligent, educated young man, in the strange months surrounding the Munich crisis. Where the later work *Autumn Sequel* seems too formal, too contrived in its verse form for its journal subject matter, *Autumn Journal* has just the right amount of formal restrictions without being contrived.

At the opposite extreme to these poems of loose, rambling form, are others of extreme precision, poems of taut, structural arrangement. These are often the short poems which MacNeice, especially in his last three volumes, could do so well. One might cite *The Lake in the Park, Restaurant Car, House on a Cliff* and many others. In a conversation with Robin Skelton, MacNeice told of his manner of writing poetry:

L

His manuscripts, Louis MacNeice says, looked rather like mosaics. A phrase at the top of the page was reflected by one at the bottom; images were written down all over the page having no apparent connection with each other. These manuscripts were worked at for weeks until all the parts fell into place, as in mosaic work, or a jigsaw puzzle. Then, the final pattern having been revealed, the poem was polished, edited, and perfected.[3]

An obvious example of such finely worked-out pattern is the tight structural organisation of poems like *Hands and Eyes* or *Godfather*.

We can note precisely the difference in structure of the kinds of poetry MacNeice wrote, if we consider two types of his descriptive poetry. The first is discursive and ruminative. A stanza from *Littoral* will make my point clear

> *The sand here looks like metal, it feels there like fur,*
> *The wind films the sand with sand;*
> *This hoary beach is burgeoning with minutiae*
> *Like a philosopher*
> *Who, thinking, makes cat's-cradles with string—or a*
> *widow*
> *Who knits for her sons but remembers a tomb in another*
> *land.*

The subject here (the beach) is evoked by a simile, cultivated almost for its own sake. In the last two lines of the stanza we almost lose sight of the sea-shore itself as the simile develops, except that the phrase 'another land' leads us back to the sea. The poem is subjective and reflective. At the other extreme, certain of MacNeice's descriptive poems are made up of numerous, short, stabbing images, or sense impressions. Such a structure at its best suggests a passive neutral eye: it suggests myriad sense impressions thrusting in on an observer. This obviously has a relationship with MacNeice's sense of the human self, isolated in a world of changing objects, cut off and separate. The world, however, thrusts itself into the consciousness by its undeniably existent, vigorous reality. The structure of some of his descriptive poems suggest this. It is as if a film-camera were panning across a landscape observing detail after detail in swift succession, to build a composite, impressionistic picture. The opening poem of *Didymus* demonstrates the point:

> *Roses and sandalwood,*
> *Red spittle on the flagstones of the temple,*
> *Green flash of parrots, phosphorescent waves,*
> *Caparisoned elephants and sacred bulls,*
> *Crystal-gazers, navel-gazers, pedants,*
> *Dazzling and jangling dancers, dazzling lepers,*
> *Begging unfingered hands and mouthing eyes,*
> *Faces on faces each like a blind end . . .*

This is an extreme example and it must be admitted that when overdone as it is in this poem, it can become an enervating technique, an irritating indulgence in a technical strategy for its own sake. But when used sparingly as in the second poem of *The Island* it can be most effective:

> *The timeworn baker,*
> *Burnt out of Smyrna, smokes his hubble-bubble,*
> *The grey stones breathe in sky, a slim and silent girl*
> *Gathers salt from the sea-crags, green among green leaves*
> *Figs, kid-soft purses, bulge, on low stone roofs*
> *Figs, grapes, tomatoes, dry in the sun and sweat*
> *Pastes the hair to the forehead . . .*

This has the immediacy of drama and the feeling of actual experience. The separate, sharp sense details, fuse to create a convincing picture; the camera flitting over the landscape has composed, apparently randomly, an impressionistic landscape of disorganised, disparate, exciting fragments. As MacNeice's thought is taut with a sense of opposites, so the structure of his verse can swing between such differing kinds.

MacNeice's frequent use of light verse forms can be seen as related to his sceptical sensibility. The sceptic distrusts portentous solemnity[4] as much as religious or political dogma, so he is playful, witty. But this does not preclude seriousness. Light verse and vigorous surrealist ballads can have deadly serious effects. The surface wit, the playful ambiguities, the jingling rhythms, are the sceptic's attempt to respond to the mystery of existence, to say at least something about it. He avoids the frontal assault, but will explore an image, play with a verse form, build a poem round a nursery-rhyme structure. Faced by the insoluble tragedy of modern life, by 'the appalling unrest of the soul', perhaps the only way to try to make sense of it is to be light, frivolous, to laugh. But laughter can express more than humour. Such poetry responds to the collapsing world with the sombre despair of a dark nursery rhyme.

> *Mass destruction, mass disease:*
> *We thank thee, Lord, upon our knees*
> *That we were born in times like these*
>
> *When with doom tumbling from the sky*
> *Each of us has an alibi*
> *For doing nothing—Let him die.*

MacNeice's wide variety of verse structures can also be related to his basic scepticism. The reader senses that the endless inventiveness, the restless experimentation in rhythm and stanza form, is a quest for an adequate mode of expression to describe the incomprehensible world. MacNeice himself suggested this as a reason for his friend, W. H. Auden's experimentation in verse forms: 'Auden in the last few years, in an attempt to do justice to the multiplicity of modern life, has tried many forms of light verse, taking hints from Skelton, from mummer's plays, from broadsheets, from American cowboy poetry, from nonsense verse, from jazz songs.'[5] In his own work at one pole, ranging discursive verse searches the inner worlds of the poet's introspection, without affirming anything dogmatic about the external world. At the other pole, tightly knit poems record vivid sensory details, in form suggestive of a self that is conscious of the vast multiplicity of the world, unable to make any affirmation about it. Between the two poles the poet searches endlessly for a form in which he can say something about the world, and sometimes all that can be arrived at is a tender, poignant lyricism. Here sad refrain and limpid verbal music are all the sceptical poet can manage.

One other important aspect of the structure of MacNeice's poems must be noted at this point. As one reads through the *Collected Poems*, especially through its later pages, one notices how many of the poems are organised round a heavy central caesura. Even if this occurs only in one line of a stanza, the reader feels that this is the basic pattern of the verse, and that the other lines are variations from the norm, which add piquancy to the verse. This must not be over emphasised, for there are a large number of poems which exhibit no traces of this structure whatsoever. The effect, however, occurs with sufficient regularity for the reader to notice it, and for it to be considered of some significance. The frequency of its occurrence seems rather more than merely coincidental. Such verse has a curious, balanced, see-saw effect, as it rocks around its caesura. A stanza from *Donegal Triptych* clearly demonstrates the point.

> *Here for instance: lanes of fuchsias*
> *Bleed such hills as, earlier mine,*
> *Vanished later; later shine*
> *More than ever, with my collusion.*

The variation in the second line rather points than breaks the balanced pattern of the verse structure: the heavy pattern having been established in line one, the reader notices the variation in line two, and is all the more aware of the original pattern when it reasserts itself in the following two lines. This effect, as with so many of the technical aspects of MacNeice's verse, is sometimes overdone. It can become rather slick, briskly mannered, as in this stanza from *April Fool*:

> *Here come I, in guts and brass,*
> *Between the raven and the pit.*
> *Fool me under, fool me flat,*
> *Coffins land on Ararat.*

This seems too easy. The verse trips along; the reader suspects that sense has been sacrificed to formal considerations. Yet the effect, when used with more subtlety, as in the previous example or in this stanza from poem three of *Suite for Recorders*—

> *Your Alter Egos, present, past,*
> *Or future even, could not last*
> *Did your word only prove them true;*
> *Though you choose them, yet they chose you . . .*

—has an important suggestive significance. It begins to suggest, as it recurs in the poetry, a poet whose sensibility naturally turned towards oppositions, polarities, as he attempted to respond to complex experiences. The dialectical predilections of his poetic sensibility receive their stylistic embodiment in a habitual recourse to a structure of balanced tensions. The treatment of the paradox of life in time in *Suite for Recorders* is consolidated by the poem's see-saw structure. Style is thought, is basic apprehension of the world.

We now turn to the study of the poet's diction, to consider what kind of words he in fact uses, and how they operate in the poems they help to create. At one extreme in the spectrum of MacNeice's diction, is the highly ostentatious, sometimes grotesque, diction of poetic bravura. This aspect of his diction has a clear relationship to the flashy, non-structural imagery which I discussed earlier and it has the same significance as the floating image. At the other end of the spectrum is a diction of an extreme simplicity, sometimes banal, at others tense and austere.

T. S. Eliot has written that 'to have the virtues of good prose is the first and minimum requirement of great poetry',[6] and surely one of the major virtues of good prose (that is, writing which fulfils the function of rational communication of subject matter) is simplicity of diction. This requires some definition. By simple diction I mean a choice of language which appears to the reader to be largely non-metaphorical. One calls that writing which seems intent upon communicating facts in statements, prose; and that writing which communicates more by metaphor, sound etc., poetry. Obviously this is a matter of degree, for all writing is, by the fact that it uses language, metaphorical. Prose is that vehicle of communication which as far as is possible, uses words to convey intellectual concepts. In prose a word stands for a concept. In poetry a word can give body to the concept by its sound and emotional content. Obviously there is no clear dividing line between the genres. It is basically a matter of degrees of transparency. Simple prose diction is transparent when the reader is unaware of the way a thing is said and is able to concentrate almost entirely on what is being said. He is able to see through the language to what is being communicated. This is of course to speak metaphorically and also ideally—totally transparent writing is an impossible abstraction, for even in the most 'transparent' prose the meaning is created by, and is present in, the verbal structure itself, not behind it somewhere. Complex metaphoric diction (which is a constituent of most poetic effects) is less transparent than prose diction, for it draws attention to itself as well as pointing to its subject matter. This can occur to varying degrees finally including both the self-referential, opaque symbolist poem, and the concrete poem where language tries to be the thing itself, to be totally free of referential content and transparency.

Much of MacNeice's verse is prosaic in the sense defined above. Of course its prosaicism consists as much in the rhythm and syntax employed, as in the diction, but the diction is a significant constituent of this effect. An early poem such as *Nature Morte* admirably displays this use of prosaic diction. It begins:

> *As those who are not athletic at breakfast day by day*
> *Employ and enjoy the sinews of other vicariously,*
> *Shielded by the upheld journal from their dream-*
>   *puncturing wives*
> *And finding in the printed word a multiplication of their*
>   *lives,*
> *So we whose senses give us things misfelt and misheard*
> *Turn also, for our adjustment, to the pretentious word . . .*

An element in the prosaicism here is the careful diction. No image is more than a faded metaphor, (except for 'dream-puncturing wives'); the diction suggests that each word and phrase has been chosen with a serious concern as to its conceptual accuracy. In poem after poem there are passages of such muted, unmetaphoric prosaicism, which communicate with a kind of sober strength. This chaste diction convinces that the poet is being honest with us. He makes no attempt to trick with windy rhetoric or overdone poeticism. One might characterise poetry of this kind as 'poetry of statement', for it achieves its effect by the use of diction (as well as the syntax and rhythms) of prose statement welded into a poem. These poems maintain the use of a language which would not disturb a prose context, yet which by subtle, almost imperceptible imagery, quickens into the indefinable condition of poetry. Thus a poem like *Hidden Ice* begins with the completely prosaic statement:

There are few songs for domesticity
For routine work, money-making or scholarship
Though these are apt for eulogy or for tragedy.

Then by a subtle use of diction suggesting clocks and chrono-
meters, the poem can sustain the fully fledged metaphoric
diction of the final stanza. For we continue to read the last stanza
as we read the first, as poetry of statement, hardly aware that we
are being confronted with complex poetic imagery (explained
by MacNeice on page 176 of his book *Modern Poetry*):

One was found like Judas kissing flowers
And one who sat between the clock and the sun
Lies like a Saint Sebastian full of arrows
Feathered from his own hobby, his pet hours.

At all stages of his poetic career MacNeice shows himself capable of writing such spare, spruce poetry, poetry almost bereft
of what is usually described as poetic diction. All the examples
cited so far are from his early poetry. One might just as well
have quoted *The Death-Wish* (1940), or the extreme simplicity
of diction used in *Autobiography* to evoke the lost world of
childhood. One might have suggested *Conversation* as a poem
which creates its effect by simple statement, in which submerged,
scarcely discernible images finally develop into full metaphor.
This poem begins with simple prosaic statements and instruc-
tion:

Ordinary people are peculiar too:
Watch the vagrant in their eyes ...

to proceed almost imperceptibly, in simple prosaic diction, to
develop the imagery of vagrancy. Even amidst the highly ornate,
indeed overly elaborated metaphoric diction of *Ten Burnt
Offerings*, the reader can come upon a passage of moving
simplicity, of chaste, spare language such as this poem in
Didymus:

And beside that sea like a sea on the moon
He clasped his hands to make sure they were only
Two and, finding them two but strong,
Raised them gently and prayed.

One could also draw attention to the prosaic diction of a later poem[7] like *Beni Hasan* with the disturbing statement:

> *It came to me on the Nile my passport lied*
> *Calling me dark who am grey.*

Yet even here the verse is not entirely non-metaphorical although it appears so. For there is evident through the poem a subtle use of simple adjectives of colour which help to create a mood; that is to say they act as substitutes for metaphoric language. The adjectives 'dark' and 'grey' begin the work which is completed when tombs are described as 'black eyes'. This subtle use of colour adjectives to act in lieu of metaphors in creating mood is a frequent ploy of many of the later poems of simple, almost prosaic, diction. In *Death of an Old Lady* the voices heard in the dank fields are 'grey voices' and April is 'grey April' while the first stanza of *The Atlantic Tunnel* uses the adjective 'black' most tellingly:

> *America was ablaze with lights*
> *Eastward the sea was black, the ship*
> *Black, not a cigarette on deck;*
> *It was like entering a zigzag tunnel.*

The diction is almost non-metaphorical by normal poetic standards yet the repetition of the word 'black' draws our attention to it, giving the poetry a potency beyond the merely descriptive. Such repetition evokes the mood, as it does in the strangely disturbing statements in a late nightmare poem:

> *The conductor's hands were* black *with money;*
> *Hold on to your ticket, he said, the inspector's*
> *Mind is* black *with suspicion . . .*
> *. . . He looked at us coldly*
> *And his eyes were dead and his hands on the oar*
> *Were* black *with obols and varicose veins . . .*
>
> (Author's emphases)

The colour adjective operates on both the descriptive and metaphorical levels, yet the diction seems plain and unadorned.

Donald Davie in his book *Purity of Diction in English Verse* has written about prosaic strength in verse, about what he calls 'nicety of statement'[8] in the following terms: 'This strength of statement is found most often in a chaste or pure diction, because it goes together with economy in metaphor; and such economy is a feature of such diction. It is achieved by judgment and taste, and it preserves the tone of the centre, a sort of urbanity.'[9] It is this tone which most often comes from those poems in which MacNeice uses plain, spare diction. They have a sort of urbanity, a kind of sophisticated yet guarded watchfulness. They give the impression of knowledge, awareness, yet do not preclude strong feeling, which is never, however, permitted to become uncontrolled. Simple diction in itself is no guarantee of poetic worth, for it may fall into the vice of banality, as it occasionally does in MacNeice's work. But used to help create this tone of accurate, urbane communication in a poetry of statement, it admirably justifies itself. This is *The Mixer*:

> *Colourless, when alone, and self-accused,*
> *He is only happy in reflected light*
> *And only real in the range of laughter;*
> *Behind his eyes are shadows of a night*
> *In Flanders but his mind long since refused*
> *To let that time intrude on what came after.*

Such writing has the virtue of good prose: strength, lucidity, and an urbanity which does not preclude feeling. It is a poetry of mature, considered statement.

Unpoetic diction signifies much else in MacNeice's poetry. Its frequent use creates meaning, is a constituent of meaning as is any aspect of poetic technique. I would argue that it must be seen as the further attempt of the sceptic to say something about the world, that same compulsion that led him to speak darkly and obliquely in parables and musical structures. For all his scepticism about language's ability to describe or affirm something more than the stuff of 'the nearer future' (*Wolves*) he was a poet nurtured in the atmosphere of the thirties, which led him to believe (for all his scepticism of that decade's political dogmas) with his fellow poets of that time, that poetry must address itself to an examination of the world, it must communicate, and that it is made of words which mean. This strain, as we have seen, runs through his criticism, and writings on poetry. In a foreword to an early collection of his poems MacNeice wrote: 'We shall not be capable of depth—of tragedy

or great poetry—until we have made sense of our world.'[10]
One way of doing this may be the exploring of an image, the
creation of the special world of a parable, but MacNeice frequently attacks the problem at a somewhat less oblique angle.
Yet he rarely treats a subject without some indirection, without
suggesting some scepticism about the possibility of the success
of a frontal assault.

MacNeice, as must be clear from the preceding chapters, tried
to write *about* the world. He was almost never content merely
to describe it on the level of surface realism. He developed towards parable and musical structure, but he also wrote about the
world in a dry prosaic style of wry plainness. He wrote a poetry
of prosaic statement and keen logic which consistently suggests
a poet of doubting honesty, a sceptic attempting to get at some
truth, aware how easily questions can be begged or false emphases
cultivated. The sceptic seeks to comment with a kind of sober
controlled sanity; he adopts a Horatian urbanity in the face of
his sense of the tragedy and mystery of life. This is all he can
honestly manage. He will prune his diction of all poeticisms, of
inflations, in the attempt to say at least something honest about
the world, or as a response of mystic reverence before the sheer
mystery of being.

Such poetry, as G. S. Fraser pointed out in *Vision and Rhetoric*
is both sceptically honest, and at the same time evasive. The
cultivated, controlled, urbane voice, the wry embodiment of a
sensibility sceptical of high-flown, dishonest rhetoric in others and
anxious not to commit the same fault himself, seems one we can
trust. He is someone we can listen to without suspicion. This
poet will tell us what he knows. Yet in the end he seems to be
sceptical even of his own ability, about the poem itself, and
we miss what we expected to hear. Richard M. Elman has
written well on this aspect of the diction in MacNeice's poetry.
He comments on the later volumes, but I should wish to apply
his words to MacNeice's work in general :

> His later poems are the work of a widely read man of wit
> and perception who tried to make the necessary connections
> between what he wrote, the way he lived, and what he read,
> and who often chose deceptively modest forms and a pellucid
> idiom of language to comment upon himself as a part of the

common weal. Sometimes this language was deliberately flat-
tened out to serve notice on the audience to respond without
romantic excess . . . And there are even times when the lucidity
seems to be about his own confusions, and when a poem
seems to proceed lucidly enough toward a point of emotional
and intellectual obscurity, a vagueness. But MacNeice never
denied there were mysteries. An early poem begins 'the
familiar rhythms but the unknown implications', and in
another poem of the same period entitled *Nature Morte* he
made a characteristic observation about the painter Chardin :

> *the appalling unrest of the soul*
> *Exudes from the dried fish and the brown jug and the*
> *bowl.*[11]

It is as if the sceptic trying to make 'the necessary connections'
finally comes to the conclusion that there may be none. The
plain, prosaic, uninflated diction, the simplicity that tries to
pare things down to essentials, the logical yet evasive syntax,
all embody and suggest a basically sceptical sensibility, a sensibility aware of the complexity of life, yet which tries to make
some sense of it, even if the absolute truth must remain unknown.

Very close to this use of plain simple diction, is MacNeice's
liking for colloquialism, cliché, tag, for, indeed, the everyday
language of our time.

In MacNeice's light verse such as *Letter to Graham and Anna*
the diction (as well as the rhythms and syntax) is that of witty
chat in verse, while sections of *Autumn Journal* are the very
stuff of everyday speech. They echo the tones of the natural
speaking voice, and are perfectly suited to the loose journalistic
mode, the diary's conversation with oneself. *Prognosis* asks,
employing everyday cliché,

> *Will his name be Jason*
> *Looking for a seaman*
> *Or a mad crusader*
> *Without rhyme or reason?*

Entirely begins colloquially

If we could get the hang of it entirely
It would take too long ...

and *Brother Fire* is a development of a colloquialism. Here the
playfulness of the diction creates a potent irony in view of the
sombre subject matter:

When our brother Fire was having his dog's day
Jumping the London streets with millions of tin cans
Clanking at his tail, we heard some shadow say

'Give the dog a bone'—and so we gave him ours ...

Epitaph for Liberal Poets begins with colloquial ease: 'If in
the latter/End—which is fairly soon—our way of life goes
west ...' and concedes later, with a cliché, that 'There is no
way out ...' *Tam Cari Capitis* meditates: 'That the world
will never be quite—what a cliché—the same again' when a
friend dies and makes of the cliché a moving tribute to a friend.
In *Autolycus* the poet sums up Shakespeare's life and our own in
an appropriate colloquialism. For Shakespeare created master-
pieces of colloquialism 'gabbing earth/Hot from Eastcheap ...'
The poem ends by acknowledging that Shakespeare like us was
'born and grew up in a fix'. In *Autumn Sequel* the ambiguous
nature of life is suggested by the use of cliché diction quite
tellingly:

The fact is this:
Tempted and tempter being hand in glove

The target that we almost hoped to miss
Is what we hit ...

(*Canto III*, author's emphases.)

but it is in this poem that the weakness of using colloquial and
cliché diction becomes most evident. One meets such weak lines
as 'What's in a peak that is not name?' and 'Some grain is better
than no chaff ...' which suggest that the poet has run out of
inspiration and has had recourse to cliché and colloquialism
rather than remaining silent.

It must be admitted that this tendency to depend too much
on cliché and colloquialism can be traced throughout Mac-
Neice's work (it becomes painful in *Autumn Sequel*). It is

evident in a poem like *Street Scene* which tries unsuccesfully to
build up an image from a snatch of popular song 'Cruising down
the River'. *Ten Burnt Offerings* often fails because we are
offered weak colloquialism, poorly altered clichés, as a substi-
tute for poetry. Phrases such as 'A tall story over a dark
sanctum . . .' and water seen as 'Ringing the jackpot of colour
out of the mountains . . .' and as 'A royal flush in the hand . . .'
are simply inadequate as poetry. The lowest ebb is reached in
this volume in a couplet from poem four of *Didymus*, 'Thomas,
Thomas, do you find/That out of sight means out of mind?'
This is feebly banal wit. Elsewhere clichés and colloquialisms are
used with great ingenuity, but they sometimes simply plaster
over the cracks of a failing inspiration.

Yet it must be added that at other times MacNeice uses
clichés and colloquial diction to remarkable effect. Particularly
effective is the slight alteration of a cliché, when we are simul-
taneously aware of the original and the alteration. Both add to
the poem. For instance in *The Mixer* we are told : 'And still as
ever popular he roams/Far and near . . .' for which the mind
naturally reads the cliché 'far and wide'. The alteration has
sharp piquancy. In the darkly satiric poem *Alcohol* MacNeice
writes :

> *The siphon stutters in the archaic night,*
> *The flesh is willing and the soul is sick . . .*

where the associated phrase 'The spirit is willing but the flesh
is weak' adds an ironic note. At other times unaltered, simple
clichés have a remarkable power in MacNeice's verse, as in
poem four of *Jigsaws* when he writes of a surgeon who operates
upon him :

> *The operation must have veered*
> *Off course, had not some nameless stranger*
> *Entering your body volunteered,*
> *Hand in glove, to share your danger.*

Here the simple cliché 'hand in glove' is strangely effective. It
functions on both the literal and metaphorical level, as if by a
kind of magic, which hauntingly captures the sheer oddness of a
surgeon entering one's body to perform an operation.

MacNeice's use of cliché is very similar to his other sceptical strategies. It too, like the parable, the musical structure, the Horatian irony, allows the poet to organise a poem without the poem implying too great claims about the truth of its order. For the cliché contains within it the suggestion of its own inadequacy. We can depend on clichés to do our thinking or we may choose not to do so, insisting on their partiality. So the sceptical poet can save himself from dogmatism.

So far in this chapter we have mainly dealt with the seemingly 'simple' in MacNeice's diction, that is, diction which acts largely (though not entirely) as it would in prose. In prose, words act by communicating their intellectual, conceptual meanings. In poetry, other aspects of the word are used in creation and communication. For a word has a sound, and a kind of physical presence, something felt and experienced when read or spoken. These qualities, when used by a poet, are a part of the means of communication. G. M. Hopkins's notes to one of his own poems will make my point clear. A stanza begins:

> *How to keep—is there any any, is there none such,*
> *nowhere known some, bow or brooch or braid or brace,*
> *lace, latch or catch or key to keep*
> *Back beauty, keep it, beauty, beauty, beauty, . . . from*
> *vanishing away?*[12]

On this the poet comments 'Back is not pretty, but it gives that feeling of physical constraint which I want.'[13] The word 'back' has been chosen not simply for its conceptual meaning but for its physical qualities, its sense of constraint, its ability to communicate by its sound.

In MacNeice's poetry one senses some of the diction has been chosen for this reason, and that it is used in this manner. Words are chosen to communicate with all their possibilities. As we noted in Part I, one of the central ideas in MacNeice's thought is the tangible, undeniable, existent, reality of the physical world. Throughout his poetry much of the diction gives this conception body and muscle. For the diction itself has a hard tangible quality, a kind of felt physical presence, when this poet writes about the world. It is, in Robert Browning's fine phrase about his own poetry, 'pregnant with thing'.[14] In the early poem *Belfast* the hard, solid diction is part of the meaning of the poem. It helps to communicate a sense of that hard northern city:

> *Down there at the end of the melancholy lough*
> *Against the lurid sky over the stained water*
> *Where hammers clang murderously on the girders*
> *Like crucifixes the gantries stand.*

By its sound and physical presence it embodies its subject. The lines:

> *I give you the smell of Norman stone, the squelch*
> *Of bog beneath your boots, the red bog-grass . . .*

with their onomatopoeic effect and strong alliterations, also have this effect in *Train to Dublin*. The diction in *Carrickfergus* has itself the heavy, sturdy actuality of the place:

> *The little boats beneath the Norman Castle,*
> *The pier shining with lumps of crystal salt;*
> *The Scotch Quarter was a line of residential houses*
> *But the Irish Quarter was a slum for the blind and*
> *halt . . .*

as it does in *Sligo and Mayo*—

> *And pullets pecking the flies from around the eyes of*
> *heifers*
> *Sitting in farmyard mud*
> *Among hydrangeas and the falling ear-rings*
> *Of fuchsias red as blood . . .*

—particularly in the opening alliteration, and the rhymed words. It has a kind of experienced, tangible quality, which allows what is being described to seem physically present. Those fuchsia flowers are real. The words at the beginning of the philosophic poem, *The Cromlech* have an almost metallic ring of particularity, of the tangible, inherent in them (of course the rhythm has its part to play in this effect):

> *From trivia of froth and pollen*
> *White tufts in the rabbit warren*
> *And every minute like a ticket*
> *Nicked and dropped, nicked and dropped . . .*

The effect is created by the short sharp syllables, the use of the i's and t's and the astringent use of consonants. In *The Cyclist* the external world is evoked in all its vigorous reality in diction which itself has a vigorous physical existence :

> *The grass boils with grasshoppers, a pebble*
> *Scutters from under the wheel and all this country*
> *Is spattered white with boys riding their heat-wave,*
> *Feet on a narrow plank and hair thrown back . . .*

where, although the effect partly depends on syntax (the high-lighted words are strong verbs) it also depends on the tangible felt quality of words like 'scutters' and 'spattered'.

Of all the techniques of poetry, alliteration probably calls attention to the physical presence of the language most clearly. When describing the world MacNeice sometimes uses this technique. It helps to body forth the subject, as in the fourth poem of *The Island* where a river is successfully evoked in diction pregnant with thing, which effect is produced by the strong alliteration :

> *Through his contrived*
> *Miniature channel he dives and prattles*
> *To puddle the powdery grooves . . .*

In a passage in *Autumn Sequel* descriptive of the Oxford colleges, the diction seems to incarnate into words the very texture of the things described :

> *I roll on*
>
> *Past walls of broken biscuit, golden gloss,*
>
> *Porridge or crumbling shortbread or burnt scone,*
> *Puma, mouldy elephant, Persian lamb,*
> *And other modes of stone . . .*
>
> *(Canto XII)*

The hard words like 'shortbread', 'porridge' and 'broken biscuit' and the formidable presence of 'golden gloss' and 'mouldy elephant' are undermined, as the college walls crumble with the ravages of time, by softer words: 'scone', 'puma' and 'Persian lamb'. Also in *Autumn Sequel* we are offered a passage of hard physical poetry, where the sharp, staccato diction captures both the tangible reality of the world and the tang of experience :

M

> *On these bare downs, the haunt of ancient man,*
> *With the turf skin-deep and the chalk showing through*
> *and the knout*
>
> *Of the hail-studded wind on each stud in my spine . . .*
> *(Canto XXII)*

Here one-syllable words and hard consonants give the language
a physical quality, suggestive of the physical experience it is
describing.

In the later poetry this physical, almost tangible diction,
although now surrounded by the language of nightmare and
semi-allegory, is still to be found, as in these two evocative
stanzas from *Donegal Triptych* :

> *Here for instance: lanes of fuchsias*
> *Bleed such hills as, earlier mine,*
> *Vanished later; later shine*
> *More than ever, with my collusion.*
>
> *And more and mine than ever, the rumpled*
> *Tigers of the bogland streams*
> *Prowl and plunge through glooms and gleams*
> *To merge their separate whims in wonder . . .*

The use of assonance and alliteration, the sheer vigour of the
diction, together with the patterning, all draw attention to the
language as an almost physical object. It is as if the language
were trying to be the thing itself—the vigorous world of nature.
J. Hillis Miller has assessed Robert Browning's verse :

> His ability to convey the 'thingness' of things, in his own
> special apprehension of it, belongs not at all to the realm of
> ideas, and yet is at once the most obvious thing about his
> verse, and, it may be, the most profound. Certain of his very
> best poems are not at all complicated thematically, but they
> succeed magnificently in expressing Browning's strong feeling
> for the density, roughness and vitality of matter.[15]

This might, with equal justice, be applied to MacNeice's poems
of place, and natural phenomena.

There is, however, a danger in this kind of diction, in that it
tends to draw attention to itself. There is a very thin dividing
line between diction which validly embodies the real tangible

world, and diction whose physical, solid 'thingness' becomes a
cloud between the reader and the subject. The diction can
become clotted and opaque. The words as physical objects take
over to the detriment of communication. The diction becomes
over-contrived, a distraction. Lines from *Autumn Sequel* ex-
emplify this:

> *That England still is with us, the hands of each*
> *Being rough with marl and sarsen, flint and clunch.*
>
> *(Canto VIII)*

Here one feels that the physical language embodies the subject matter, but also that the technique is rather contrived. One
becomes rather too much aware of the words themselves.

This is the opposite extreme from the plain, simple language
with which we began this discussion of MacNeice's diction, and it
seems remarkable to find two such extremes in the one poet.
Yet this overly physical diction is also akin to (and is often
synonymous with) a kind of ostentatious bravura diction, which
occurs in MacNeice's poetry, at almost all stages of his career.
It of course occurs most noticeably in his early volume *Blind
Fireworks* (which the poet later repudiated by excluding the
greater part of its contents from his *Collected Poems* of 1949)
but it is observable in many other parts of his work. In a stanza
from *Train to Dublin* one meets:

> *And I give you the sea and yet again the sea's*
> *Tumultuous marble,*
> *With Thor's thunder or taking his ease akimbo,*
> *Lumbering torso . . .*

Perhaps such words as 'tumultuous marble', 'Thor's thunder'
'akimbo' and 'lumbering' are selected for their impressiveness
—one might argue that this conveys the majestic impressiveness
of the sea. Yet one has uneasy suspicions.

Ostentation is a frequent fault in *Autumn Sequel* where the
diction often seems too flashy, too contrived, as in this passage
of flamboyant bravura, which finally repels:

> *Acrasia grieves*
> *Her fluorescent joys, her papier mâché rocks,*
> *. . . .*
> *And all her inanimate creatures. Antirrhinums and phlox*

> *Have yielded to candy floss, the heavy fantastic*
> *Toes have tripped on a coconut, the last*
> *Fun of the fair will snap with a snap of elastic*
>
> *And all this summer's fandango be part of the past*
> *With Vauxhall Gardens and Ranelagh.*
>
> (*Canto X*)

One admires the poet's exuberance and skill, but one senses that he has nothing much to say, while the words distract from what little he has to communicate as he escapes into mere artifice.

Yet not all the bravura diction in MacNeice's poetry is non-structural and unsatisfactory. At times it can be brilliantly effective. In *Relics,* the rather grotesque language of :

> *Astrakhan rustication of the arches*
> *Puts a small world in quotes . . .*

can be seen to embody the Gothic architecture of the Oxford Colleges, while the hotch-potch of diction in *Autolycus* seems to capture the mixture of styles and forms which makes Shakespeare's last plays so enchanting :

> *Eclectic always, now extravagant,*
> *Sighting his matter through a timeless prism*
> *He ranged his classical bric-à-brac in grottos*
> *Where knights of Ancient Greece had Latin mottoes*
> *And fishermen their flapjacks—none should want*
> *Colour for lack of an anachronism.*

This conjunction of 'grottos' with 'flapjacks' is ostentatious yet successful, almost because of its daring, in suggesting the odd but fascinating eclecticism of Shakespeare's romances. In a poem such as *Flowers in the Interval* MacNeice allows his diction to bubble over, to sparkle magnificently, as suggestive of the rapture of love. I particularly like this passage from poem three—

> *Because your colours are onyx and cantaloupe,*
> *Wet seaweed, lizard, lilac, tiger-moth*
> *And olive groves and beech-woods, because you scoop*
>
> *The sun up in your hands, because your form*
> *Is bevelled hills which neither crane nor stoop,*
> *Because your voice is carved of jade yet warm*
>
> *And always is itself and always new . . .*

—where the extravagant, sparkling diction conveys an exuberant gay celebration of love. The gaiety is largely suggested by the diction. In many other poems, often love poems, the diction sparkles with the brilliance of cut diamonds. In *Mayfly* we meet the flashing lines:

> *The yokels tilt their pewters and the foam*
> *Flowers in the sun beside the jewelled water.*
> *Daughter of the South, call the sunbeams home*
> *To nest between your breasts. The kingcups*
> *Ephemeral are gay gulps of laughter.*

Comment on this would be clumsily destructive as it would in the same poem where the mayfly is seen to

> *Inconsequently dance above the dazzling wave . . .*

MacNeice's delight in the brilliance of language and the world is caught in such diction. Light flashes from the very words themselves, like sun on water, evoking the whole delightful world of sense impressions. Much of the solid, muscular thingness, even sometimes the grotesqueness of the diction and patterning is an embodiment, an incarnation of this undeniably existent world, and a revelation of the poet's relish for it. The dazzling sparkle of the diction embodies

> *Whatever it is that jigs and gleams—*
> *. . . .*
> *Viz. life.*

It incarnates by the mystery of language the vigorous tangible world, valuable by its very existence, flaunting itself before the forces of non-being and death. From the hard solidity of the diction suggestive of the physical actuality of place in *Carrick-fergus* to the dazzle with which he presents the flashing of light on water (*The Return*), the dancing of a mayfly (*Mayfly*), and the relish for the tangerine's and the rose's vital self-existent reality (*Snow*), one senses in the diction of MacNeice's verse, the real world in all its vigorous fecundity, its transient richness.

At the same end of the spectrum of diction as this bravura sparkling language, is the last major aspect of MacNeice's diction which I intend to discuss. This aspect is the poet's liking for

diction which contains a paradox, for the oxymoron, and for
diction which creates polarities. Such language tends to draw
attention to itself as does the bravura diction, in a way that the
'simple' diction, discussed earlier, does not. It must be added,
however, that these paradoxes, oxymorons and polarities sometimes appear in contexts where the language seems deceptively
plain.

Clearly this liking for paradox can be associated with Mac-
Neice's conception of life as dialectical, and also with his basic
scepticism. Life is complex, perhaps incomprehensible. The only
way to deal with it in language is to use diction which creates
the complex figure of an oxymoron, or creates a paradox, or
reflects polarities. One must demonstrate that there are opposites
at war in every situation. MacNeice himself makes this connection
(and it suggests to me that I am not unwise in making others)
of his liking for linguistic paradox with his basic view of life,
in a footnote to the already much quoted article 'Experiences
with Images'. To the passage in which he states 'My basic
conception of life being dialectical . . .'[16] he adds the footnote : 'Hence my fairly frequent use of oxymoron, the phrase
which concentrates a paradox.'[17]

This kind of diction occurs with remarkable frequency
throughout the poetry. One can only give examples from all
stages of MacNeice's poetic career to demonstrate the point. The
following examples of oxymoron, near-oxymoron and paradox,
are taken from all parts of the *Collected Poems*. We meet 'small
eternity', 'mild bravado', 'metabolism of death', 'triumphantly
self-degraded', 'oxymoron of parasitical glory', 'tops of topless
towers', 'the nearness of remoteness', 'the last way out that leads
not out but in', 'Conditioned to think freely', 'eucharist of
crime', 'change prevails', 'glad sad poetry of departure', 'being
of the water earthy', 'the permanence of what passes', 'unim-
mediately apparent', 'my far-near country', 'great mean city',
'coffinlike cradle' as well as a host of other phrases that concentrate a paradox. The effect of such diction is to suggest that
strange, dialectical complexity of life, which is part of the
subject of many of the poems.

The use of oxymorons such as these is surpassed by the use of
diction which creates (without necessarily concentrating) polarities and opposites. Frequently poems consist of words used in a

playful game to create paradoxes. A passage from *Homage to Clichés* makes this point clear,

> *This year next year sometime never*
> *Next year is this year sometime is next time, never is*
> *sometime* . . .

as does the poem *The Here-and-Never* where the diction has been chosen to create a fantasia of paradoxes and polarities. I quote the fourth stanza (note the deceptive simplicity of the diction):

> *Here it was living and dying, but never*
> *Lifelong dying or dead-alive.*
> *Few were few but all knew all,*
> *The all were few and therefore many,*
> *Landscape and seascape at one's call,*
> *The senses five or more than five.*

Again one can only give highly selective examples from the legion of instances in which MacNeice's diction seems to have been chosen to create oppositions. The ending of *An Eclogue for Christmas* opposes 'ephemeral' and 'permanent' in the lines:

> *Let all these so ephemeral things*
> *Be somehow permanent like the swallow's tangent wings*
> . . .

Meeting Point glorifies the paradox that

> *Time was away and she was here* . . .

In *Aubade for Infants* word play is used to create a polarity of concepts 'Something large/Is barging *up* and *down* . . . (my italics) while in stanza three of *Epitaph for Liberal Poets* we find a paradoxical pairing of opposites in the lines:

> *Catullus*
> *Went down young, gave place to those who were born*
> *old*
> . . . .
> *Though our songs*
> *Were not so warm as his, our fate is no less cold* . . .

as in the concluding lines of *The Window*:

> *Here is profit where was loss*
> *And what was dross is golden* . . .

and in poem three of *Suite for Recorders* :

> *Pride in your history is pride*
> *In living what your fathers died* . . .

MacNeice's fascination for paradox and polar opposites is evident even in descriptive verse, in poem four of *The Island* where we read :

> *The round of dark has a lip of light,*
> *The dams of sleep are large with daybreak,*
> *Sleeping cocks are primed to crow* . . .

or in *Indian Village* where we meet :

> *And hunkered peasants gaze beyond*
> *Their hookahs at that orb of blood*
>
> *Which* founders *towards its* rising *day* . . .

(Author's emphases.)

This fascination for paradox and polarity, at its best, has a compelling suggestiveness of the complexity and ambiguity of experience. The diction embodies an attitude which admits the multifarious complexity, the incorrigible plurality of the world, or indeed its tragic ambiguity. This one meets in a brilliant stanza from *The Grey Ones* where the poet meditates on three creatures of mythic dimensions who

> *check the client next to die,*
>
> *Who might be in some mountain cup*
> *Where climbers meet it struggling* up
> *Or might be in some Eastern town*
> *Where most men take it lying* down . . .

(Author's emphases.)

or in *Spring Cleaning* where

> *Typewriters ring, opinions wilt* . . .

and where we are presented with

> *Blain and dazzle together, together*
> *Magnolia in bloom and holly in berry* . . .

or in *Rechauffé* :

> *These* live *men filing past inspect*
> *These* dead *that serve by turns* . . .
>
> (Author's emphases.)

Nothing is simple, everything is dialectical, such paradoxes suggest as is, finally, life itself, attacked and sustained by death. Life and death are the ultimate polarities in MacNeice's diction, as in his thought :

> *Time*
> *Swings on the poles of* death
> *And the latitude and the longitude of* life
> *Are fixed by* death . . .
>
> (Author's emphases.)

As the reader notices the paradoxes and polarities in the diction of MacNeice's verse, he also must become aware of the verbal patterns of the verse. For instance, the polarities often seem to be deliberately pointed out by alliteration or internal rhyme, as in the simple example :

> *Justice undone but honours new*
> *Who came to* blight *but stayed to* bless . . .
>
> (Author's emphases.)

Here the opposing attitudes are forcibly brought to the reader's attention by the verbal pattern. Internal rhyme has the same effect in a poem like *Apple Blossom* in the line :

> *But the first verdict seemed the worst verdict* . . .

The fact that the near polarities 'first' and 'worst' create an internal rhyme adds a certain piquancy to their opposition.

MacNeice's verse is highly patterned in its language as well as its forms. Some of the patterning is of the kind Hopkins employed so frequently in his verse. Indeed it is not too great an assumption to assert that MacNeice probably learnt of the possibilities of such experiment from Hopkins. For it was in the thirties that Hopkins became acknowledged as the important poet that he is. In the thirties F. R. Leavis wrote his manifesto-like essay on Hopkins in *New Bearings In English Poetry*, while MacNeice himself wrote favourably of the Jesuit poet in *Modern*

Poetry: a Personal Essay, and contributed a penetrating piece on his work to *New Verse* in 1935.[18] In Hopkins's patterning rhyme and half-rhyme words are juxtaposed so that they seem to generate each other by a process of organic dynamism. An early poem by MacNeice, *Homage to Clichés,* contains phrases in the Hopkins mode, where both sound and sense are in parallel and the rhymed words seem organically linked, 'this gloom, this womb of stone'. Other examples occur throughout MacNeice's work but Hopkins's influence is most clearly evident in the early verse.[19] Often, however, the patterning, while founded on internal rhyming and half-rhyming, has a very different effect to that it has in Hopkins's poetry. In *A Toast* this can be seen. The opening lines are highly patterned :

> *The* luck *and* pluck *and* plunge *of blood,*
> *The* wealth *and* spilth *and* sport *of* breath . . .
>
> (Author's emphases.)

Each alliterated and rhymed word here, is cut off from its fellow. Because of their positioning in the line, and the rhythmic pointing, the words do not seem to grow out of one another, as they do in Hopkinsesque language. Rather, one senses that the words have been chosen to fit an architectural structure. The poem begins to seem like a piece of chiselled sculpture, a cut shaped stone. We see this in the lines from the poem :

> *The* face *and* grace *and* muscle *of* man
> *The* balance *of his* body *and* mind . . .
>
> (Author's emphases.)

or in lines from *Letter from India* :

> *Where smiling, sidling, cuddling hookahs,*
> *They breed and broil, breed and brawl* . . .

In this second example the verbal pattern, which is pointed out by (and also points to) the see-saw verse pattern, tends to draw attention to the poem as object.

In *Aubade for Infants,* the poem as a piece of verbal sculpturing takes over almost completely from the poem as communication. The poem's meaning is obscured by too obvious an attempt to create internal rhymes. I quote two stanzas to demonstrate :

Beyond that wall *what things* befall?
My eye *can* fly *though* I *must* crawl.
Dance *and dazzle—Something* bright
Ignites *the dumps of sodden* cloud,
Loud *and laughing, a fiery* face . . .

Whose broad grimace (*the voice is* bass)
Makes nonsense of my time and place—
Maybe you think that I am young?
I who flung *before my* birth
*To mothe*r earth *the dawn-song too!*

(Author's emphases.)

The same kind of sculptured verbal patterning is used with great effect in one of MacNeice's best lyrics. In *The Sunlight on the Garden* the complex verbal structure does not seem to interfere with the transmission of the sense, but rather seems to embody something integral, essential to the poem's meaning. I quote the first stanza to demonstrate the verbal pattern:

The sunlight on the garden
Hardens *and grows* cold,
We cannot cage the minute
Within its *nets of* gold,
When all is told
We cannot beg for pardon.

(Author's emphases.)

This intricate pattern is maintained through each of the poem's four stanzas, yet it does not obtrude itself on the reader to the detriment of sense as does the more obviously (yet less highly) patterned structure of *Aubade for Infants*. In a review of Edward Lear's *Tea Pots and Quails* MacNeice quoted favourably some words of W. H. Auden. 'As Auden wrote of Tennyson and Baudelaire: "It may well be, I think, that the more he (the poet) is conscious of an inner disorder and dread, the more value he will place on tidiness in the work as a defence . . ." '[20] This is well said, and it applies equally to MacNeice's own poem. We feel that although we cannot cage the minutes within nets of gold, at least the poet has been able to cage his feelings about it, within the filaments of a verbal pattern. Something has been done.[21] An object has been shaped of the chaos of experience, from the fear of impending doom. Thus the poem's verbal structure, its pattern, helps in the total communication which is the poem's meaning.

But the meaning of MacNeice's sculptured objects is not always stoicism. At other times his tendency to sculpt his poems is, I feel, more related to his compulsion to produce parables, musical structures, poems of ironic watchfulness, paradox or semi-cliché response. For the statement of a sculptured object is as capable of conceptual ambiguity as the parable, or symphony. Yet again, the poem as special world directs the reader's attention away from the poem as communication about the real world. Sometimes this created special world, the chiselled object, does communicate the sceptic's stoicism in the face of the tragic dimensions of experience (as in *The Sunlight on the Garden,*) but often verbal organisations become opaque and narcissistic. They do not seem to point to anything beyond themselves. They self-consciously consider their own verbal structures. This tendency in MacNeice's poetry is an embodiment of the poet's scepticism of his ability to say anything important about reality at all. This scepticism of language as a means of communication, explicitly stated as it is in a poem such as *Babel*, receives its formal embodiment in poems which attempt to explore images, create special worlds, and sculpt verbal artifices. Such poems may or may *not* have a relationship of meaning with reality.

7

Scepticism: Its Syntax and its Tone

DOUGLAS Sealy has written of MacNeice's poetry: 'Though he told us so much about his life, he seems to have withheld some part of himself. He did not create a mask or persona; he did not strut as an actor before an audience, but spoke as a man; he respected another man's privacy and demanded respect for his own.'[1] It is this feeling which G. S. Fraser expresses by the phrase, 'the sense that a good deal is held in reserve' and by the brilliant oxymoron, 'Evasive Honesty', which he entitles his chapter on MacNeice in *Vision and Rhetoric*. For in reading MacNeice we are tormented by the feeling that he is being completely honest with us and yet that he is not telling us anything. He speaks to us as man to man, and yet we sense that he is withholding something. He tells us honestly of himself and yet he evades us. If we examine his poetry we see that this feeling of his honesty is very largely a result of certain syntactical measures.[2] Primary among these is the widespread use of parenthesis.

Time and time again MacNeice will interrupt the flow of his poetry to include a phrase in parenthesis, to qualify what he is saying. This creates the impression that what the poet is interested in is honesty, accuracy at all costs, and devil take the poetry. MacNeice wrote of the poet's need for honesty. In a note to *Autumn Journal* he tells us 'But poetry in my opinion must be honest before anything else and I refuse to be "objective" or clear-cut at the cost of honesty.' He might have added that he refused to be rhetorical or 'poetical' at the cost of honesty. He further wrote in 1948: 'The thirties poets, the so-called "social consciousness" poets, quite often overplayed their hand and lapsed into mere propaganda, and by this I mean that they stated an opinion or introduced an image not because it came from their experiences, but because it was the thing to do. But a poet should never, never, never, fake his reactions.'³ What if a parenthesis mars the music of a line, the poet will at least be honest. Parenthesis is used throughout the poetry to clarify, to cut down to size, to avoid inflated and dishonest pretension. In *Epitaph for Liberal Poets*, we see the deflationary honest use of parenthesis at work when the poet questions :

> *What,* though better unsaid, *would we have history say*
> *Of us who walked in our sleep and died on our Quest?*
> (Author's emphases.)

and concludes with brutal honesty created by the parenthesis :

> *we shall vanish first,*
> *Yet leave behind us certain frozen words*
> *Which some day,* though not certainly, *may melt*
> *And,* for a moment or two, *accentuate a thirst.*
> (Author's emphases.)

We see a similar ironic deflationary honesty in the syntactical structure at the end of *The Springboard* :

> *He will dive like a bomber past the broken steeple,*
> *One man wiping out his own original sin*
> *And,* like ten million others, *dying for the people.*
> (Author's emphases.)

In the last stanza of *The Casualty* the use of a double parenthesis again suggests an extreme honesty, a desire to tell the whole truth :

> *the fact remains*
> (Which I, for all your doubts, could have no doubt of)
> *That your whole life till then showed an endeavour*
> *Towards a discovery.*
> (Author's emphases.)

In *To the Public* the technique is used with an honest, self-depreciatory irony where he writes of poets as a species :

> *Who,* legislators or not, *ourselves are lawless* . . .
> (Author's emphases.)

In *Beni Hasan* it creates a sense of sudden, terrifying self-realisation, in a sombre irony. The row of tombs in a brown cliff is like :

> *black eyes on eyes that stared away*
> *Lion-like focused on some different day*
> *On which,* on a long-term view, *it was I, not they, had*
> *died.*
>
> (Author's emphases.)

In the first poem of *Notes for a biography* he writes

> *An oranges (sweet) and lemons (bitter) childhood* . . .

explaining his images in parenthesis as if he is afraid that he will be misunderstood. We sense from the syntax his desire to communicate, to get across his meaning, while in the second poem of the series the parentheses suggest a tentative, doubtful approach to his subject. It is as if the poet is aware of the ambiguity of his subject, and is concerned not to misrepresent anything :

> *Splinters under the nails, weals on the buttocks,*
> *Schooled to service (or was it pride of class?)*
> . . . .
> *Until the pass was sold (or was it redeemed?)* . . .

Sleeping Winds suggests by its syntax the honest scepticism of a man who is unprepared to commit himself either way :

> *she never stirred*
> *Till Brandan joined his hands and,* coincidence or not,
> *She got on her knees and filled her lungs and put*
> *Her lips to the sail and puffed.*
>
> (Author's emphases.)

Here the parenthesis produces a tone like that of a storyteller who breaks off from his tale to inform his hearers that he is not quite sure of the truth of his tale, and in all honesty he must remind them that it may be apocryphal. In *The Blasphemies* parenthesis suggests simply a total honesty, an openness to admit his human limitations :

> *nor can he longer*
> *Speak for the world*—or himself—*at forty* . . .
>
> (Author's emphases.)

while in *Nature Notes* the syntactical device is used to create verse of logical accuracy, a verse of sane, considered distinctions :

Cats

> *Incorrigible, uncommitted,*
> *They leavened the long flat hours of my childhood,*
> *Subtle*, the opposite of dogs,
> *And*, unlike dogs, *capable*
> *Of flirting, falling, and yawning anywhere* . . .
>
> (Author's emphases.)

This poem, as well as employing parenthesis, develops with syntactical care. Indeed it moves with the tense yet cautious syntax of the lecture room. MacNeice wrote in 1957 'I like to think that my latest short poems are on the whole more concentrated and better organised than my earlier ones, relying more on syntax and bony feature than on bloom or frill or the floating image.'[4] Earlier we noticed how MacNeice's use of imagery became more structural as time went on. We can also see an increased reliance on taut logical syntax in his later verse. Yet this tendency to use what I shall call lecture-room syntax was always present in MacNeice's verse. *Museums* (1933) begins like a lecture on the subject :

> *Museums offer us, running from among the buses*
> *A centrally heated refuge, parquet floors and sarco-*
> *phaguses* . . .

A poem of 1940 is of the same kind. *The Death-Wish* begins with a statement, which creates a sense of taut, controlled logic :

> *It being in this life forbidden to move*
> *Too lightly, people, over-cautious, contrive*
> *To save their lives by weighting them with dead*
> *Habits, hopes, beliefs, anything not alive* . . .

From this basic premise the poet develops logically :

> *Which being so, it is not surprising that*
> *Some in their impatience jump the rails* . . .

The phrase 'which being so' is like a lecturer reaffirming his premise and yet honestly reminding his hearers that it is a premise, and not a proven fact. *Autolycus* begins like a lecture on Shakespeare :

> *In his last phase when hardly bothering*
> *To be a dramatist, the Master turned away*
> *From his taut plots and complex characters*
> *To tapestried romances* . . .

though the poem breaks away from this tone. The opening poem of *Suite for Recorders* has a logical development which suggests discursive argument :

> *If shepherd to nymph were the whole story*
> *Dying in holocausts of blossom,*
> *No midwife and no middleman*
> *Would contravene the upright sun.*

It is however in the poet's last three volumes that this kind of logical, lecture-room syntax becomes most prevalent. Poem three of *Donegal Triptych* begins :

> *Which being so, which beauties being evanescent but also*
> *   recurrent,*
> *And Fate, frustrating, fulfilling, turning the screw,*
> *It is good to pause on the turn* . . .

while even a dark nightmare-like poem *Figure of Eight*, manages its connectives by lecture syntax :

> *He chose to wait.*
> *No one came. He need not perhaps have worried.*

> *Whereas today in the rear and gloom of a train,*
> *Loath, loath to meet his fate, he cowers and prays* . . .
> (Author's emphases.)

Poem six of *Visitations* is syntactically like a lecture on poetics :

N

> *So those who carry this birthright and this burden*
> *Regardless of all else must always listen ...*

while *On The Four Masters* chooses 'Ancient Ireland; modern attitudes to,' for its subject. This poem even has the lecturer's joke in parenthesis, a topical rather weak reference to the Gaelic League. *Icebergs* proceeds in tight logical stages. The first stanza considers a possibility, a theory—

> *If icebergs were warm below the water*
> *. . . .*
> *They still might signal all was well ...*

—which the rest of the poem sets out to destroy. The lecturer has set up a straw man as a means of making his point :

> *But icebergs are cold in the dark water,*
> *Cold their base as white their crest ...*

In the last stanza the lecturer rather unfairly attacks those who took his straw man too seriously :

> *the rest is sheer*
> *Snub to those who dared suppose*
> *Icebergs warm below the water.*

Perspectives also develops with the logical syntax of the lecture room. It begins with a premise :

> *The further-off people are the smaller ...*

for which a number of examples are cited. But the honest lecturer will also cite possible refutations of his premise, and leave the listeners to make up their own minds :

> *Yet sometimes for all these rules of perspective*
> *. . . .*
> *The further-off people are sometimes the larger.*

The effect of this lecture-room syntax in MacNeice's verse is ambivalent. It paradoxically suggests a kind of honesty, and also the sense of something held in reserve. One has the sense that one has with any good lecturer, that he has a wide command of his subject and that he is trying to select his words honestly so as not to misrepresent the case. But one always feels that there is much else he could say if he had the time and the conviction.

One wonders is this the whole case, or only as much as the lecturer is willing to commit himself to at present in view of the vast complexity of the subject. One senses that the lecturer is respecting the conventions and not wearing his heart on his sleeve. He is a lecturer, and must keep a certain distance from his audience. This syntactical habit (which is also a habit of attitude) partly accounts for the strong sense of 'evasive honesty' that one derives from MacNeice's poetry.

The sense of something held in reserve can also be attributed to MacNeice's frequent habit of paring away the non-essential syntactical units of a linguistic structure. This creates a kind of notebook poetry. It is as if what the reader is presented with is not the total poem, but notes to it. If he had had the inclination to write out the whole poem, the poet would have included more material. Strangely this technique does not simply mean that the poems seem unfinished. Rather, it seems to give to them a suggestiveness of a depth which cannot be articulated. They seem like the top of a mysterious iceberg. What is revealed is important, glittering in the sunshine, or coldly warning of danger, but we sense that the submerged depths might sink the ship. *Plant and Phantom* is a case in point. It begins simply, like a notebook jotting :

> *Man: a flutter of pages,*
> *Leaves in the Sibyl's cave . . .*

and we feel that were it written out in full there might be more to it, though what has been given is a highly adequate indication. *Perdita* begins in the same way with a *collage* of notebook jottings, without any attempt at a full, normal, syntactical arrangement :

> *The glamour of the end attic, the smell of old*
> *Leather trunks—Perdita, where have you been*
> *Hiding all these years?*

In *Ten Burnt Offerings* this technique can become rather irritating, where, as with so many other aspects of technique in that volume, one senses that the poet is simply substituting technique for the felt thought which is poetry. Here the notebook phrases seem simply notebook phrases and do not suggest the important nine-tenths of the iceberg lurking beneath the surface. The verse is almost all surface. A section from poem one of *Areopagus* will demonstrate :

> *A tall story over a dark sanctum:*
> *That Hebrew riddling in a land of olives*
> *Was an appetiser for a tired mind.*
> *With a stone in it too. A sharp titillation*
> *With a snub, if not threat, in it too.*

The notebook phrases suggest a sophisticated tourist's journal and the technique seems dangerously like a mannerism indulged in for lack of any more satisfactory alternative :

> *Limestone burning the feet, and opposite*
> *Tiers of Pentelic, he whetted the blade*
> *Of the wit of his faith to slice their pagan*
> *Prides to the quick; they nudged and doubted.*
> *Diamond cut diamond. Something new.*

The notebook phrases create no resonances here as they do in some other poems where we sense that the elliptical phrases are a gnomic, concentrated attempt to sum up much deeply felt consideration of a difficult subject. Here the iceberg is only its visible one-tenth.

The notebook technique is used to fine effect in *Sailing Orders*. I quote from the first stanza :

> *Gangway or Curtain Up! Then forth*
> *We move—white horses, amber lights—*
> *Towards coral islands of first love*
> *Where makebelieving boy and girl*
> *Assume the magic of the spheres.*

The scene is set with notebook phrases, like brief stage directions, and they bring into the poem associations which provide the poem with a depth beyond the immediately discernible. Our memories of the excitement of a new play or our first boat journey are tapped and drawn on in the simple notebook phrases 'Gangway or Curtain Up!' and 'white horses, amber lights', and we sense that, had the poet cared to, he could have expanded this association between the boat journey and the new play. Instead he keeps it at the notebook level throughout the poem. Yet strangely this is enough, for the poem persuades us to do the poet's work of expansion for him, and in a sense this is more effective than if he had made everything specific in developed metaphors. The sense of something held in reserve contributes positively to the value of the poem. We meet this notebook poetry, where syntax is pared of its non-essentials, in stanzas like this from *Country Week-End* :

> *So now it is time. Decant the oil,*
> *Turn up the wick. Call it escape*
> *Or what rude name you like—or call it*
> *A good deed, rather a good night:*
> *One good night in a naughty world.*

Here the syntax is simplified (being cast in the imperative) suggesting that complex ideas are being enumerated in swift, gnomic, notebook phrases. *Sunday in the Park* begins with similar sharp, staccato notebook phrases which suggest unplumbed depths of meaning held in reserve :

> *No sunlight ever. Bleak trees whisper ironies,*
> *Carolina duck and Canada goose forget*
> *Their world across the water . . .*

The Blasphemies is a kind of notebook biography and achieves its effect by the sense of what is left unsaid as well as what is said :

> *The sin against the Holy . . . though what*
> *He wondered was it? Cold in his bed*
> *He thought: If I think those words I know*
> *Yet must not be thinking—Come to the hurdle*
> *And I shall be damned through thinking Damn—*
> *But whom? But no! Those words are unthinkable;*
> *Damn anyone else, but once I—No,*
> *Here lies the unforgivable blasphemy.*

Sports Page also sets a scene with notebook phrases which bring to mind all we associate with the games of our childhood, and gives the poem hidden depth, so that it can sustain the heavy moral at the end :

> *Nostalgia, incantation, escape,*
> *Courts and fields of the Ever Young:*
> *On your Marks! En Garde! Scrum Down! Over!*
> *On the ropes, on the ice, breasting the tape.*

The associations of school games, created by the notebook evocation of them, are coupled with suggestions of myth in the phrase 'Courts and fields of the Ever Young', and given added depth by the single words 'Nostalgia, incantation, escape' which set the mood, and also suggest that much else might be said. The unseen nine-tenths of the iceberg is there, giving added dimension and power to the poem.

The notebook poetry, by the fact that it does not seem to state a whole case, helps to create the feeling of evasiveness in MacNeice's verse. The poet is willing to state so much; there remains much also which might be said, but which the poet is chary of committing to paper. We sense the existence of the submerged part of the iceberg but are unable to describe its exact nature. It is as if what happens below the surface is the poet's own affair.

This sense of evasiveness is heightened by another very frequent and simply effective syntactical ploy. This is MacNeice's use of the bare third-person pronoun when writing about people (including himself). This occurs throughout his verse and it suggests a certain indirectness of approach to his subject, as if the poet knows the name of his subject but is unwilling to divulge it. Time and time again, even when the poem is (from our knowledge of the poet's life) obviously biographical, he adopts the bare, indirect use of 'he'. Particularly, when the exegetical knowledge that the poem is autobiographical, is to hand, this approach has a strange air of evasiveness about it. One feels that if the poet wished he could come clean and tell us the name and livelihood of his character, or tell us that he is writing about himself. This he does not do. He keeps his distance, keeps the reader at arm's length by the indirectness of his syntactical approach to his subject. One might offer numerous examples from all periods of his work, but I restrict myself to one (*The Truisms*) which shall be representative of the rest :

His father gave him a box of truisms
Shaped like a coffin, then his father died;
The truisms remained on the mantelpiece
As wooden as the playbox they had been packed in
Or that other his father skulked inside.

Then he left home, left the truisms behind him
Still on the mantelpiece, met love, met war,
Sordor, disappointment, defeat, betrayal,
Till through disbeliefs he arrived at a house
He could not remember seeing before,

And he walked straight in; and it was where he had come
from
And something told him the way to behave.
He raised his hand and blessed his home;
The truisms flew and perched on his shoulders
And a tall tree sprouted from his father's grave.

The use of the third person pronoun (together with the use of simple diction and the lack of any specific detail) suggests to the reader that he is being told the bare minimum. The poet knows more than he is telling us, but withholds for his own good reasons. These we cannot discover, but the withholding of the information in fact gives the poem an anonymity, a universality which makes it a more powerful achievement than if it had been couched in the first person and had been full of personal detail. The fact that the poet holds something in reserve is a potent factor in the poem's effectiveness. To insist that a poet wear his heart upon his sleeve is to set up criteria for poetry which have no validity and which, if observed, may in fact produce inferior work.

This evasiveness that we have noted in MacNeice's poetry (which together with the sense of honesty is largely created by subtle techniques of syntax) can be associated, like all the technical habits studied in this part of the book, with MacNeice's basically sceptical attitude which plays such a part in his basic thought. It is a kind of tonal embodiment of it. As one reads through his verse, the feeling of honest evasion tends to suggest a poet who only rarely commits himself and who is always aware that there may be much else to be said on a subject, that there are always at least two points of view to everything.

Conclusion

Live man and dead
Being each unique
(Their pain and glory),
Yet some will have left
By force or freak
To us the bereft
Some richer story;
Their say being said,
They still can speak
Worlds more unique
More live, less dead.

(Visitations)

WHETHER such an outlook of fundamental scepticism is sufficient for the creation of great poetry, we must wait for posterity to judge. Yet the question, major or minor? is largely irrelevant to us at present. All one can say is that (in David Holbrook's words) 'In full maturity the responsible poet may attain an assurance of voice which has itself a metaphorical power—taking us into his confidence in human nature—something we could never have attained by ourselves.'[1] MacNeice attained that maturity and that assurance of voice. His poetic contribution to our literature is the embodiment of a creative scepticism in a verse, and therefore in a voice, which is nearly always recognisably and maturely his own. In his verse we share his sceptic's 'confidence in human nature' and more fully in life itself, something one doubts whether we could have attained ourselves.

In *Memorial Stanzas for Louis MacNeice* George Barker wrote:

Thus I would like to hope
The ironic Horatian
Ode that in its scope
Looks no larger than
A pocket telescope
Taught your verse to scan
The dying skies of Europe
With the eye of a man . . .[2]

This to me seems a fitting epitaph for the poet of sceptical vision.

Select Bibliography

PUBLISHED BOOKS BY LOUIS MACNEICE

Blind Fireworks, London: Gollancz, 1929.

Roundabout Way, London: Putnam, 1932. Published under the pseudonym 'Louis Malone'.

Poems, London: Faber and New York: Random House, 1937.

The Agamemnon of Aeschylus, London: Faber, 1936 and New York: Harcourt, Brace, 1937.

Out of the Picture: A play in two acts, London: Faber, 1937, and New York: Harcourt, Brace, 1938.

Letters from Iceland, with W. H. Auden, London: Faber and New York: Random House, 1937.

I Crossed the Minch, London: Longmans, 1938.

Zoo, London: Michael Joseph, 1938.

Modern Poetry: A Personal Essay, London and New York: Oxford University Press, 1938; second edition with a Foreword by Walter Allen,1968.

The Earth Compels, Poems, London: Faber, 1938.

Autumn Journal, London: Faber and New York: Random House, 1939.

The Last Ditch, Dublin: Cuala Press, 1940.

Selected Poems, London: Faber, 1940.

Poems, 1925–1940, New York: Random House, 1940.

Plant and Phantom, London: Faber, 1941.

The Poetry of W. B. Yeats, London and New York: Oxford University Press, 1941; second edition with a Foreword by Richard Ellman, London: Faber, 1967.

Meet the U.S. Army, prepared for the Board of Education by the Ministry of Information, London, 1943.

Springboard, Poems 1941–44, London: Faber, 1944 and New York: Random House, 1945.

Christopher Columbus: A Radio Play, London: Faber, 1944; second edition for schools with new Introduction, 1963.

The Dark Tower and other Radio Scripts, London: Faber, 1947; second edition of *The Dark Tower*, 1964.

Holes in the Sky, Poems 1944–47, London: Faber and New York: Random House, 1948.

Collected Poems 1925–48, London: Faber and New York: Oxford University Press, 1949.

Goethe's Faust, Parts I and II, translated by MacNeice in association with E. L. Stahl, London: Faber, 1951 (second edition, 1965) and New York: Oxford University Press, 1952.

Ten Burnt Offerings, London: Faber, 1952 and New York: Oxford University Press, 1953.

Autumn Sequel, London: Faber, 1954.

The Other Wing, London: Faber, 1954.

The Penny that Rolled Away, New York: Putnam, 1954: second edition as *The Sixpence that Rolled Away*, London: Faber, 1956.

Visitations, London: Faber, 1957 and New York: Oxford University Press, 1958.

Eighty-five Poems, selected by the author, London: Faber and New York: Oxford University Press, 1959.

Solstices, London: Faber and New York: Oxford University Press, 1961.

The Burning Perch, London: Faber and New York: Oxford University Press, 1963.

The Mad Islands and the Administrator: Two Radio Plays, London: Faber, 1964.

Astrology, London: Aldus Books in association with W. H. Allen, 1964, re-issue by Spring Books, 1966.

The Strings are False, London: Faber, 1965.

Varieties of Parable, Cambridge: at the University Press, 1965.

Collected Poems, edited by E. R. Dodds, London: Faber, 1966, and New York: Oxford University Press, 1967.

One for the Grave, London: Faber, 1968.

Persons from Porlock and other Plays for Radio, with an Introduction by W. H. Auden, London: B.B.C. Publications, 1969.

A bibliography of Louis MacNeice can be found in the *Bulletin of Bibliography and Magazine Notes*, Vol. 27, nos. 2 and 3, 1970. It was contributed by William McKinnon. *See also* Christopher Armitage and Neil Clark, *A Bibliography of the Works of Louis MacNeice*, London: Kaye and Ward, 1973.

SOME CRITICAL STUDIES OF MACNEICE

Walter Allen, 'Louis MacNeice', *Essays by Divers Hands*, Vol. 35, 1969, 1-17.

G. S. Fraser, 'Evasive Honesty', *Vision and Rhetoric*, London: Faber, 1959.

Ian Hamilton, 'Louis MacNeice', *A Poetry Chronicle*, London: Faber, 1973.

William T. McKinnon, *Apollo's Blended Dream*, Oxford University Press, 1971.

D. B. Moore, *The Poetry of Louis MacNeice*, Leicester University Press, 1972.

John Press, *Louis MacNeice*, London: Longmans, Green and Co. for the British Council, 1965.

Elton Edward Smith, *Louis MacNeice*, New York: Twayne Publishers, Inc., 1970.

J. Southworth, *Sowing the Spring*, Oxford: B. Blackwell, 1940 (chapter on Lewis, Spender, MacNeice).

Notes

ABBREVIATIONS

C.P.   *The Collected Poems of Louis MacNeice*, ed. E. R. Dodds, London 1966 and New York 1967.
E.W.I.   Louis MacNeice, 'Experiences with Images', *Orpheus II* (1949)
M.P..   Louis MacNeice, *Modern Poetry: A Personal Essay*, London and New York 1938.
S.A.F.   Louis MacNeice, *The Strings are False*, ed. E. R. Dodds, London 1966
V.O.P.   Louis MacNeice, *Varieties of Parable*, London 1965.
W.B.Y.   Louis MacNeice *The Poetry of W. B. Yeats*, London and New York 1941.

FOREWORD   (pp. 1–4)

1. Anthony Thwaite, *Contemporary English Poetry*, London: Heinemann 1959, 85. Mr. Thwaite has subsequently reconsidered this opinion.
2.William McKinnon's *Apollo's Blended Dream*, Oxford University Press, 1971, was the first substantial study of MacNeice's poetry to take MacNeice seriously (perhaps too seriously) as a thinker and his book provided many useful insights and pieces of information about MacNeice's writing. However, I would disagree with him as to the nature of MacNeice's philosophic position, as this study will make plain. Mr. McKinnon's book furthermore tended to portray MacNeice as more philosopher than poet, failing to suggest how much a poet's concern with metaphysics is intuitive, even unconscious, rather than systematic. His book also failed to convince that he valued the poetry as poetry, for all the care and usefulness of his pioneering research.

THE ROOTS OF ART: A BIOGRAPHICAL INTRODUCTION   (pp. 5–28).

1. E. R. Dodds, editor, in Louis MacNeice, *The Strings are False*, London: Faber and Faber, 1966, 15. Henceforth S.A.F.
2. S.A.F., 43.   3. S.A.F., 151–2.   4. S.A.F., 241.

5. Desmond Pacey, 'The Dance Above the Dazzling Wave', *Transactions of the Royal Society of Canada*, Vol. III, Series IV (June 1965), 153.

6. Louis MacNeice, *The Poetry of W. B. Yeats*, London and New York : Oxford University Press, 1941, 47. Henceforth W.B.Y.

7. Stephen Gwynn, *Experiences of a Literary Man*, London : Butterworth, 1926, 11.

8. S.A.F., 226. 9. S.A.F., 228. 10. S.A.F., 230.

11. S.A.F., 112. 12. S.A.F., 78–9.

13. Roy McFadden, 'Review of Louis MacNeice's *Collected Poems*', *Rann*, 7 (Winter 1949–50), 11.

14. S.A.F., 222.

15. Michael Roberts, *Critique of Poetry*, London : Cape, 1934, 238.

16. S.A.F., 104. 17. S.A.F., 101.

18. He also knew, as an Irishman, that men were capable of 'Shooting straight in the cause of crooked thinking/Their greed . . . sugared with pretence of public spirit.' *Eclogue from Iceland*.

19. J. F. MacNeice, *Carrickfergus and its Contacts*, London 1928, 66.

20. *Ibid.*, 73. 21. *Ibid.*, 72. 22. *Ibid.*, 83–4. 23. S.A.F., 54–5.

24. S.A.F., 243–4. 25. S.A.F., 54. 26. S.A.F., 101.

27. S.A.F., 233.

28. Louis MacNeice, *Modern Poetry: a Personal Essay*, London and New York : Oxford University Press, 1938, 198. Henceforth M.P.

29. M.P., 62. 30. W.B.Y., 230. 31. W.B.Y., 231. 32. *Ibid.*

33. M.P., 201. 34. W.B.Y., 7. 35. S.A.F., 38. 36. S.A.F., 216.

37. S.A.F., 53–4.

CHAPTER 1. MISUNDERSTOOD ROMANTIC
(pp. 31–45).

1. Others did. See John Bayley, *The Romantic Survival*, London : Constable, 1957.

2. Louis MacNeice, *Varieties of Parable*, Cambridge : at the University Press, 1965, 51–2. Henceforth V.O.P.

3. MacNeice's unpublished radio play, *One Eye Wild* (first broadcast 1952, rebroadcast 1961) dramatises a number of very similar situations of dream and disillusionment.

4. Quoted by F. L. Lucas in his *The Decline and Fall of the Romantic Ideal*, Cambridge : at the University Press, 1963, 125.

5. Quoted by C. K. Stead in his *The New Poetic*, London : Hutchinson, 1964, 22.

6. Frank Kermode, *Romantic Image*, London : Routledge and Kegan Paul, 1961, 145.

7. S.A.F., 43. 8. M.P., 34.

CHAPTER 2. THE MODERN SENSIBILITY
(pp. 46–77).

1. Anthony Thwaite, *Contemporary English Poetry*, 88.
2. J. Hillis Miller, *The Disappearance of God*, London : Oxford University Press, 1963, 10–11.
3. Thomas Altizer, quoted by Thomas Ogletree in his *The Death of God Controversy*, London : S.C.M. Press, 1966, 61.
4. Stephen Spender, *Poetry Since* 1939, London : The British Council, 1946, 28. For Spender's further remarks on the period, see *World Within World* (1951) and *The Creative Element* (1953).
5. W. H. Auden, 'Louis MacNeice', *Encounter*, Vol. XXI, No. 5 (November 1963), 48.
6. Stephen Spender in *New Signatures*, ed. Michael Roberts, London : The Hogarth Press, 1932, 91.
7. *Ibid.*, 86.
8. Graham Greene, quoted by Julian Symons in his *The Thirties*, London : The Cresset Press, 1960, 26.
9. S.A.F., 134.   10. W.B.Y., 96.
11. Louis MacNeice, 'When I was Twenty-One' *Saturday Book* (1961), 234.
12. F. O. Matthiessen in *The Responsibilities of the Critic*, ed. John Rackcliffe, New York : Oxford University Press, 1952, 108–9.
13. MacNeice tells us of the nature of his sympathy for the Left in *The Strings are False* : 'The strongest appeal of the Communist Party was that it demanded sacrifice; you had to sink your ego. . . . I had a certain hankering to sink my ego, but was repelled by the priggishness of the Comrades and suspected that their positive programme was vitiated by wishful thinking and over-simplification. I joined them however in their hatred of the *status quo*, I wanted to smash the aquarium.' S.A.F. 146.
14. Louis MacNeice, *The Mad Islands and the Administrator: Two Radio Plays*, London : Faber and Faber, 1964, 43.
15. Louis MacNeice, *One for the Grave*, London : Faber and Faber, 1968, 57.
16. Louis MacNeice, 'The Ould Opionioneer', *New Statesman*, Vol. LXV, No. 1677 (3 May 1963), 679.
17. Iris Murdoch, *Sartre*, London : Collins, 1967, 36.
18. W. H. Auden, *The Enchaféd Flood*, London : Faber and Faber, 1951, 56–7.
19. John Bayley, *The Romantic Survival*, 9–10.
20. Ibid., 41.   21. Miller, *op.cit.*, 8.   22. V.O.P., 93.
23. V.O.P., 94.   24. M.P., 64.
25. It is, however, not even desirable. In *The Strings are False,* MacNeice wrote : 'Man cannot live by courage, technique, *imagination* alone. He has to have a sanction from outside himself. Otherwise his technical achievements, his empires of stocks and

shares, his exploitation of power, his sexual conquests. . . . are merely the self-assertion, the self-indulgence of a limited self that whimpers behind the curtains, a spiritual masturbation.' S.A.F., 173 (my italics). It is interesting further that one of the temptations the hero of *The Dark Tower* must resist is the temptation to escape into a solipsistic world. In the play, solipsism as an escape from the difficulties of the real world is represented by The Soak. Of that character MacNeice wrote in a note : ' "The Soak" I should have called Solipsist if that word were known to the public. His alcoholism is an effect rather than a cause.' *The Dark Tower and Other Radio Scripts,* London : Faber and Faber, 1947, 197.

26. Dylan Thomas, *Collested Poems,* London : J. M. Dent and Sons Ltd., 1952, 58.

27. *The Collected Poems of W. B. Yeats,* London : Macmillan, 1961, 62.

28. Editor's Preface to *The Collected Poems of Louis MacNeice.*

CHAPTER 3. SCEPTICAL FAITH (pp. 78–98).

1. Or seems to be, for such systems create their own problems.
2. S.A.F., 124–5.   3. S.A.F., 125.
4. MacNeice expressed the same thought in an unpublished article when he wrote with reference to dramatic form : 'Aristotle was primarily a biologist and he thinks of a play as an organism. But he thought of organism in teleological terms. Organic life "finds its nature"—his favourite phrase—in the differentiation of species. An individual plant "finds its nature" in its development from seed to flower.' 'Unities in the Drama', 29 August 1938. (Read in MS.)
5. S.A.F., 119.
6. It can also be discerned in his various prose writings. For instance in an unpublished article he wrote of the Communist Party : 'The Communist Party have become the collectors of fossils. "Yes" they say, "we're Communists. It's the only logical thing to be." But life cannot be solved by logic. Any more than Higher Mathematics can teach one to swim.' Louis MacNeice, *Broken Windows or Thinking Aloud,* c.1940. (Read in MS.) To the Irrationalist life can never be solved by logic. A further passage written in 1940 is full of Irrationalist assumptions and responses : 'Man's deference to any logic of black-and-white, of all or nothing, is probably due to his basic illogicality; he just cannot cope with the world in colour. He refuses to distinguish conditions from causes. He cannot recognise the importance of the Economic Factor without trying to split the atom with it. A leopard cannot change his spots but a man, having divided the world into sheep and goats, can always become a sheep overnight.' Louis MacNeice, 'The Poet in England Today', *New Republic* (25 March 1940), 412.

7. In the fragmentary but interesting unpublished article *Broken Windows or Thinking Aloud,* already referred to, MacNeice wrote words which fill out the lines quoted : 'Death in its own right—as War does incidentally—sets our lives in perspective. Every man's funeral is his own, just as people are lonely in their lives, but death as a leveller also unites us in life and death, not only levels but differentiates—it crystallises our deeds. We did not need a war to teach us this but war has taught us. Before the war we wore blinkers. Applied science by increasing comfort and controlling disease, had —geared to a "liberal" individualism—encouraged us to think of death as a pure negation, a nuisance. But applied science, by shattering a town overnight, by superimposing upon ordered decay a fantastic but palpable madness, has shown us the integral function of death. Death is the opposite of decay; a stimulus, a necessary horizon'.

8. Louis MacNeice, 'London Letter'. (Typescript.)

9. W.B.Y., vii.

10. MacNeice described another such occurrence in a passage in his article, 'When I was Twenty-One' : 'When I was drunk, I found, things could either look more so, themselves with added emphasis, or swoop off into fantasy and look like quite other things; in either case the change seemed an improvement. I also noticed that, on a morning after, something very simple, like an earthenware pot of flowers or the clock across the quad or an earthenware pot empty, could fill my whole consciousness like a solid meal—or was this perhaps going for a ride on a tiger, was the thing perceived making a meal of me?' Louis MacNeice, 'When I was Twenty-One', *Saturday Book* (1961), 236–7.

CHAPTER 4. THE POET AND HIS IMAGERY
(pp. 101–24).

1. Robin Skelton, *The Poetic Pattern,* London : Routledge and Kegan Paul, 1956, 169.

2. *Ibid.,* 170.

3. T. S. Eliot also thought that it does : 'Only a part of an author's imagery comes from his reading. It comes from the whole of his sensitive life since early childhood.' John Hayward, ed., *T. S. Eliot Selected Prose,* London : Peregrine Books, 1963, 89.

4. On this subject, Scots poet Hugh MacDiarmid is interesting. In an article entitled *Growing up in Langholm* he wrote : 'There is a place at Langholm called the Curly Snake where a winding path coils up through a copse till it reaches the level whence, after passing through a field or two, it runs into the splendid woods of the Langfall. It has always haunted my imagination and has probably constituted itself as the ground plan of my mind, just as the place called the Nook of the Nights Path in Griboshov, the great forest

o

north of Hillerod, haunted Kierkegaard's.' Hugh MacDiarmid, 'Growing up in Langholm', *The Listener,* Vol. 78, No. 2003 (17 August 1967), 205.

    5. V.O.P., 12.

    6. It also occurs in MacNeice's plays. See *The Dark Tower, Christopher Columbus, The Mad Islands* and *The March Hare Sagas.*

    7. Nevertheless in order to give some indication of their frequency, here is a list of titles in which the train image is used as a major trope of a poem : *Trains in the Distance* (C.P., 3), *Train to Dublin* (C.P., 27–8), *Trilogy for X* (C.P., 88–91), frequent usage in *Autumn Journal* and *Autumn Sequel, Corner seat* (C.P., 218), *Slow Movement* (C.P., 237–8), *Figure of Eight* (C.P., 463), *Restaurant Car* (C.P., 504), *Star-Gazer* (C.P., 544). In many other poems the image is suggested, but in each of these titles it is developed at some length. MacNeice tells us that as a child railways had always been for him a symbol of escape. The passage reads (he is writing of the sea) : 'it was a symbol of escape. So was the railway which ran a few hundred yards below our house. . . .' Louis MacNeice, 'Experiences with Images', *Orpheus II* (1949), 127. (Henceforth E.W.I.) The train always carries us to new surroundings.

    8. This interpretation of the flowing river, of running water representing a change integral to value, in MacNeice's thought, is enforced by a passage from *The Strings are False.* There MacNeice wrote 'Plato had thought he was condemning the bodily pleasures when he compared them to the pouring of water through a sieve. I was willing to accept this comparison but argued that life is like that; life is like water and water must always be on the move, it is the only way it can realise its value; see for yourself, put a rose on your watering can and water your garden, see the pattern and prismatic colours of the water in the air. For pattern is value and a *static* pattern dies on you.' S.A.F., 127. It is in this ever-moving stream that we seek the

> *Divined but never known—the evasive universal;*
>   *For fumbling after the scent*
> *Dissolved in the running water of time we fool our fancy*
> *To catch intact what always is in dispersal.*

Louis MacNeice, *Departure Platform* in *The Last Ditch,* Dublin : Cuala Press, 1940, 20.

    9. S.A.F., 126.

    10. Graham Shephard was 'Drowned on active service 1943 (c.f. "The Casualty", *Springboard* p. 41), he appears as Gavin in *Autumn Sequel,* Canto II', Editor's note to *The Strings are False.* C.f. the radio play *He had a Date,* a very moving dramatic account of Shepherd's life.

11. E.W.I., 128.

12. Louis MacNeice, 'Childhood Memories', *The Listener*, Vol. LXX, No. 1811 (December 1963), 990.

13. *Saturday Book*, 1961, 237–8.   14. E.W.I., 126.

15. For example in *The Stygian Banks* Section III :

> *What when the wind blows and the bough breaks?*
> *Will each life seem a lullaby cut off*
> *And no humanity adult.*

The genesis of such imagery can be seen in a detail of MacNeice's biography. He relates an incident of his childhood in *The Strings are False* : 'In the spring I committed a murder. Down in the hedge by the bottom walk in the garden, where my mother used to walk with my sister, there was a bird's nest. I could hear the little birds cheeping but the nest was too high for me to see into, so when no one was around I reached up for it and it capsized. I cannot remember seeing the nestlings fall out, but when I came past there again, there they were hanging in the hedge, little naked corpses, terrible, silent.' S.A.F., 55. This could explain the close association with death that the cradle falling from a tree has in MacNeice's poetry. It helps to explain what is a rather private image. The writer for one had never associated the nursery-rhyme incident with death.

16. This attitude may also have its genesis in MacNeice's childhood experience. He tells us in *The Strings are False* 'And Annie the cook had a riddle which began "What is it that goes round and round the house?" And the answer was the wind but, though I knew that was the answer in the riddle, I had a clammy suspicion that in fact it might be something else. Going round and round the house, evil, waiting to get me.' S.A.F.,38. The wind is often thought of as something to be feared in MacNeice's poetry.

17. E.W.I., 129.

18. Louis MacNeice, 'A Modern Odyssey, *New Statesman*, Vol. LX, No. 1553 (17 December 1960), 979.

19. *Poetry Book Society Selection*, No. 38 (September 1963).

20. Louis MacNeice, *Zoo*, London : Michael Joseph, 1938, 40–41.

21. The flickering flight of the mayfly occurs a number of times in MacNeice's work as an image of the ephemeral beauty of the world. Apart from this example we meet it in *The Dark Tower* with 'The mayflies jigging above us in the delight/Of the dying instant', in *Suite for Recorders* where the lives of the Elizabethans are 'Mayflies in a silver web which dangled over chaos', and in *Memoranda to Horace* where the poet's monument, raised against the world is 'Weaker and less of note than a mayfly'.

CHAPTER 5. THE IMAGE IN THE POEM AND THE
POEM IN THE WORLD (pp. 125–50).

1. G. S. Fraser, *Vision and Rhetoric*, London : Faber and Faber
1959, 186.
2. In *The Arts Today*, ed. G. Grigson, London : John Lane, The
Bodley Head, 1935, 64.
3. *Ibid.*, 66.
4. Louis MacNeice, 'A Statement', *New Verse*, Nos. 31–2 (Autumn
1938), 7.
5. Louis MacNeice, 'Subject in Modern Poetry', *Essays and
Studies of the English Association*, Vol. XXII (1936), 144.
6. *Ibid.*, 145.   7. *Ibid.*, 144.
8. Louis MacNeice, 'Poetry, the Public and the Critic', *New
Statesman*, Vol. XXXVIII, No. 970 (8 October 1949), 381.
9. Louis MacNeice, W.B.Y., 38.   10. M.P., 4–5.   11. W.B.Y., 4.
12. Quoted in M.P., 64.
13. Louis MacNeice, Introduction to *Blind Fireworks*, London :
Gollancz, 1929.
14. M.P., 47.   15. E.W.I., 130.   16. *Ibid.*
17. C. Day Lewis, *The Poetic Image*, London : Cape, 1947, 1965,
99–100.
18. E.W.I., 130.   19. *Ibid.*   20. *Ibid.*   21. E.W.I., 131.
22. E.W.I., 132.   23. *Ibid.*   24. *Ibid.*
25. 'Unities in the Drama', 29 August 1938. (MS.)
26. E.W.I., 130.
27. Louis MacNeice, *Christopher Columbus*, London : Faber and
Faber, 1944, 11.
28. Louis MacNeice, 'Books in General', *New Statesman*, Vol.
XLIV, No. 1123 (13 September 1952), 293.
29. Louis MacNeice, reviewing *George Herbert* by Margaret
Bottral and *George Herbert* by Joseph H. Summers, in *The London
Magazine*, Vol. 1, No. 7 (August 1954), 74.
30. Michael Longley, 'A Misrepresented Poet', *Dublin Magazine*, Vol. 6, No. 1 (Spring 1967), 70.
31. E.W.I., 131.   32. *Ibid.*   33. *Ibid.*
34. E.W.I., 132. This has obvious affinities with T. S. Eliot's
thinking in his essay 'The Music of Poetry' : 'The use of recurrent
themes is as natural to poetry as to music. There are possibilities
for verse which bear some analogy to the development of a theme
by different groups of instruments; there are possibilities of transi-
tions in a poem comparable to the different movements of a symphony or a quartet; there are possibilities of contrapuntal arrangement of subject-matter.' John Hayward, ed., *Selected Prose, T. S.
Eliot*, 63.
35. Edwin Honig, *Dark Conceit*, London : Faber and Faber, 1960,
113.

36. Northrop Frye, *Anatomy of Criticism*, Princeton : The University Press, 1957, 193.

37. Graham Hough, 'The Allegorical Circle', *The Critical Quarterly*, Vol. 3, No. 3 (Autumn 1691), 202.

38. V.O.P., 130. 39. *Ibid*. 40. V.O.P., 6.

41. In *The Arts Today*, 66.

42. W.B.Y., 135. 43. W.B.Y., 214.

44. Louis MacNeice, *The Dark Tower and Other Radio Scripts*, 21.

45. Louis MacNeice, 'Poetry, the Public and the Critic', *New Statesman and Nation*, Vol. XXXVIII, No. 970 (8 October 1949), 381.

46. E.W.I., 131. 47. V.O.P., 7–8. 48. E.W.I., 131.

49. MacNeice wrote in a note to his volume *Solstices* that 'These forty-odd poems include . . . a large number of overt and covert parables.' *Poetry Book Society Bulletin*, No. 28 (February 1961).

50. V.O.P., 28. 51. *Ibid*. 52. V.O.P., 8.

53. Louis MacNeice, *Poetry Book Society Bulletin*, No. 28 (February 1961).

54. *The Dark Tower*, 21. 55. *Ibid*, 22. 56. V.O.P., 122.

57. V.O.P., 134. 58. V.O.P., 151.

59. John Holloway, 'The Modernity of Edwin Muir', *The Colours of Clarity*, London : Routledge and Kegan Paul, 1964, 98.

60. *Ibid*., 107–8. 61. *Ibid*., 99.

62. MacNeice once wrote at Oxford : 'we understand that all art is theatrical and that the success of the piece depends not on an accurate likeness to anything off the stage but on a self-contained coherence upon it (which artificial coherence naturally corresponds to some desire or potentiality in nature previously unsatisfied).' Quoted in M.P., 66. Here we see an early understanding of art's special world, a world that does not necessarily mirror a coherence fully developed in the real world.

CHAPTER 6. SCEPTICISM: ITS LANGUAGE AND ITS FORMS (pp. 151–82).

1. For instance the lament for Dylan Thomas (Canto XX) of which Michael Longley has written that it 'is one of the loveliest long poems in modern poetry'. Michael Longley, 'Misrepresented Poet', *Dublin Magazine*, Vol. 6, No. 1 (Spring 1967), 73.

2. N.B. W. H. Auden's introduction to *The Oxford Book of Light Verse* and MacNeice's own remarks 'Some intensely serious poetry has a streak of lightness in it, while there is little "light verse" which has not a serious undertone, however tiny.' M.P., 179. MacNeice thought of Horace's Odes as examples of such serious light verse.

3. Skelton, *op. cit.*, 25.

4. The late George McCann who knew MacNeice well told me that this was a characteristic of the man as well as of the poet. For documentation of this see George McCann, 'Louis MacNeice : a recollection', *The Northern Review*, Vol. 1, No. 2, 61–6.

5. M.P., 190.

6. Quoted by Donald Davie, *Purity of Diction in English Verse*, London : Chatto and Windus, 1952, 27.

7. N.B. MacNeice wrote of one of his later volumes 'Several poems in *Solstices*, e.g. *Country week-end*, were deliberate exercises in simplicity or at least in a penny-plain technique where fancy rhythms and rhymes would not obtrude too much.' *Poetry Book Society Bulletin*, No. 28 (February 1961).

8. Davie, *op. cit.*, 67.

9. *Ibid.*, 68.

10. Quoted by Babette Deutsch, *Poetry in our Time*, New York : Columbia University Press, 1956, 399.

11. Richard Elman, 'The Legacy of Louis MacNeice', *The New Republic* (26 October 1963), 19.

12. *The Poems and Prose of Gerard Manley Hopkins*, ed. W. H. Gardner, Harmondsworth : Penguin 1953, 52.

13. Quoted by F. R. Leavis, *New Bearings in English Poetry*, 141.

14. Quoted by J. Hillis Miller, *The Disappearance of God*, 118.

15. J. Hillis Miller, *The Disappearance of God*, 123.

16. E.W.I., 126.   17. *Ibid.*

18. See Louis MacNeice, 'A Comment', *New Verse*, No. 14 (April 1935).

19. Babette Deutsch has noticed the particular influence of Hopkins on MacNeice : 'The first poets to heed Hopkins's lessons were those whose chief theme was not the spiritual drought of the solitary, but the shame of a social class that had refused or abused the responsibilites of power. There are traces of his influence throughout Auden's early verse, and the same poet has sounded clearer echoes than Hopkins of the rhythms of *Piers Plowman*, a poem that he had cited as warrant for his own practice. Appreciation of Hopkins's technique is attested by Louis MacNeice's more turbulent rhythms and more conspicuous sound patterns, especially in his onomatopoeic pieces on air bombardment.' Babette Deutsch, *Poetry in our Time*, 303.

20. Louis MacNeice, 'He Weeps by the Side of the Ocean', *New Statesman*, Vol. XLVI, No. 1187 (5 December 1953), 721.

21. To this one might add MacNeice's remarks in an unpublished article : 'The "message" of a work of art may appear itself to be defeatist, negative, nihilist; the work of art itself is always *positive*. A poem in praise of suicide is an act of homage to life.' *Broken Windows or Thinking Aloud*, c.1940. (Read in MS.) See his statement, in a review, that Wilfred Owen's feeling for form 'redeems his most despairing poems from passivity just as Hopkins's

architectonics had redeemed his Terrible Sonnets.' Louis Mac-
Niece, 'Out of Ugliness', *New Statesman*, Vol. LX, No. 1545
(22 October 1960), 624.

CHAPTER 7. SCEPTICISM: ITS SYNTAX AND ITS
TONE (pp. 183–93).

1. Douglas Sealy, 'Louis MacNeice', *The Dubliner* (Spring
1964), 31.
2. MacNeice himself understood the importance of syntax. In the
last review he wrote he emphasised the importance of syntax in
verse. 'I have often been surprised that reviewers of verse pay so
little attention to syntax. A sentence in prose is struck like a golf-
ball; a sentence in verse can be treated like a ball in a squash
court. Frost, as Brewer brings out, is a master of angles.' Louis
MacNeice, 'Frost', *New Statesman*, Vol. LXVI, No. 1687 (12 July
1963), 46.
3. Louis MacNeice, 'English Poetry To-day', *The Listener*, Vol.
XL, no. 1023 (2 September 1948), 347.
4. *Poetry Book Society Bulletin*, No. 14 (May 1957).

CONCLUSION (pp. 194–5).

1. David Holbrook, *Llareggub Revisited*, London: Chatto and
Windus, 1962, 69.
2. George Baker, 'Memorial Stanzas for Louis MacNeice,' *Poetry*,
Vol. CIV, No. 1 (April 1964).

Index